The
Nearest
Poem
Anthology

Edited by **Sofia M. Starnes**
POET LAUREATE OF VIRGINIA, 2012-2014

Cedar Creek Publishing
A Virginia Publisher of Virginia Books
Bremo Bluff, VA 23022
www.cedarcreekauthors.com

Printed in the United States of America

Library of Congress Control Number 2014931156

ISBN 978-0-9891465-0-0

Contents

Emotion

Meaning

Poetry Matters: An Introduction

He was an old mystic-poet, imagination's ideal eidetic man; I was a story-telling, word-wielding child. He lived in London, a city I would visit some three decades later, on my honeymoon, long after I'd left the Manila of my 1960s childhood. William Blake's childhood had unfolded some 200 years earlier, in the 1760s.

Blake lived in the pages of my English textbook. The text did not tell me much about him, or about the angels that (I later learned) he would see—or sense—on the trees around his London home. If I'd heard about those angels as a child, the "news" would not have seemed too strange or outlandish.

My parents bought our textbooks a week or so before the school year started, and I would thumb through them in curious anticipation. It was then—not in a classroom setting—that I read these verses from "Auguries of Innocence":

> To see a World in a Grain of Sand
> And a Heaven in a Wild Flower
> Hold Infinity in the palm of your hand
> And Eternity in an hour....

The verses seem almost naïve today, in our unbelieving age—yet they are no less dear or wise. From them, as a child, I learned a rather profound truth: that everything is knowable and that the clues to knowledge are all around us. What's more, we often embody them. Suddenly, to say, *I can know everything!* had become a well-founded hope.

These verses had another effect on me: they led me to see that the intelligibility of things is as intrinsic to poetry as it is to other intellectual and scientific endeavors. When poets contemplate things, we start by seeing them for what they are, in order that we might see what they evoke. We use words not only to define precise reality, but also to suggest other realities. In fact, as I soon realized, words are sadly limited in their power to define or contain reality; yet, they are virtually limitless in their potential to suggest. Like water eddying in a pond, knowledge through poetry is immediate yet ultimately inexhaustible.

⤙⤙⤙

Inexhaustible. I have been urged to be less "grandiose" when speaking of poetry, less challenging. We mustn't intimidate possible readers with what poetry is capable of awakening in them. Nor must we discourage would-be poets by demanding from them more than they—or we—might be capable of creating. Satisfaction with sincere effort may be enough. To these intimations I can think of no better answer than the one my mother might have given, and she was the wisest person I've ever known: *It is sad to ask for gold and receive only silver; it is far, far sadder to ask for silver when we might have had gold.*

Fear of poetry, like holy fear, means reverence that enthralls, and reverence never disregards the miniature icon, the handheld sacramental, the symbol on a string. It does not stifle our potential or scare the wits out of genius. It recognizes the power of meekness and of the journey encapsulated in every step. We learn that the small, unassuming poem has greater depth and reach than we might assume. Still waters run deep—as the cliché goes—yet, rippling brooks are likely to take moonlight farther.

Think of it this way. Unless we're tragically afflicted with hydrophobia, it is impossible not to love the water. Even those who fear the ocean are likely to stand on the beach and let the water tease their toes. Or, held farther back through dread of the unknown, we will yet contemplate the inhale and exhale of the waves, the ineffable expression of their life, the horizon both permanent and altered by the making and unmaking of each day. Holding on to our residue of awe, we return to the quiet shelter of our homes: drink a glass of water, take a shower, simmer the broth of a bouillabaisse, sprinkle salt on a dish of clams. Both proximity and smallness are now enhanced by the trace-reverence we've carried with us indoors, reverence for a source and a destiny that lie beyond us.

ᔪᔭᔪ

When I'm asked to explain why poetry matters—yes, the kind with inexhaustible potential—I consider poets like Blake for whom *beauty* was essential. As was *emotion*. And *meaning*. This is the triune scaffolding on which great poetry rests.

Poetry supposes *beauty*, which is the coherence between internal and external reality. We find a rose beautiful, because there is something in us that responds to its colors, its symmetry, its intangible grace, all of which produce intense pleasure. The rose is true, and we respond to it through a sharing of that truth. If we lose the truth of ourselves, we will lose the truth of what is outside ourselves.

Poetry allows us to see ourselves as we are and the world as it truly is. It goes beyond appearances into the true nature of things, and thus it allows beauty to occur. Even in the direst circumstance, this commitment to truth, to honesty, brings beauty into an experience. And not surprisingly, poetry invariably shows that a human being is indeed a beautiful "thing"—for it is a true thing—and that the world, truly, *is* a thing of beauty.

Then there's *emotion*. Poetry is reduced to discourse if it does not trigger an emotional response in the reader. We exist in relation to ourselves and to the other. Poetry awakens this awareness in us; it engages us by spurring the need to move out of ourselves. This outward journey—or sojourn—is what we call emotion; only through emotion can we be fully engaged with the world around us.

Finally, poetry presumes *meaning*, because human beings are purposeful creatures. When confronted with chaos or randomness, we ask what, we ask why, we ask with whom, and we ask what for. We would not ask these questions if we did not carry in us, at the very least, the trace elements of meaning.

It is not the business of poetry to answer large existential questions in an argumentative manner, the way a philosopher or a theologian might. Poets are often at home in mystery. Yet, by virtue of creative engagement, poetry makes **its case** for meaning—regardless of how hidden (or "slant", as Emily Dickinson might say) that meaning might be. By remaking reality into words and utterances, sounds and silences, poetry aligns herself with sense, with substance. If the world—whether an ephemeral hibiscus or a stalwart oak, a brief afternoon siesta or enduring death—is worth writing about, it is because it means something to us. A stone in a poem is an uttering stone; it most definitely has something to say.

And so we have these three: beauty, emotion, meaning. For this reason, the 112 poems in *The Nearest Poem Anthology* have been arranged into three sections, each section meant to be an invitation to seek out a particular response. In reality, the division is quite arbitrary. How could it not be, since there is constant, communicative overlap in all the poems, and the trinity is present throughout the collection? After all, there is emotion in our response to beauty, and beauty may be the best arbiter of meaning. Still, the idea behind this trifurcation is that what one seeks, one finds. I invite you to take whichever road you wish, and look.

క్రోక్రోక్రో

The Nearest Poem Anthology is not a "hit parade" of poems, nor is it a selection of our most popular poets. Once a poem is written, the poet recedes—powerless to do more—and the poem must rely on a reader for its survival. It is the reader's response to a poem that guarantees its life.

The anthology is, therefore, a testament to the multiple lives of poetry, its constant reincarnation. A poem may remain dormant for a while—decades, even centuries—and then someone picks it up, takes it to heart, finds in its words and nuances echoes of a personal experience. And the poem finds a new birth.

Most readers probably have several nearest poems, poems they have approached intimately, tangibly, at different moments of their lives. For the purpose of this anthology, all contributors have selected and submitted only one. The brief essay that accompanies each poem explains their decisions by sharing a response to the poem, how the poem has been reborn in them.

I have endeavored to feature submissions from as many localities as possible across the Commonwealth (the name of each contributor and his or her city of residence appear after each selection). I have also tried to include as wide a variety of backgrounds, professions, avocations, and ages as I could, limited only by the entries I received. The youngest contributor is 12 years old; the oldest, in her mid-90s. Not surprisingly, given my home's location, a notable percentage of the submissions have come from the Tidewater area, and I am grateful to all these "local" readers who responded so generously to my call for submissions. My only regret is that I have been unable to include every one of them, because of space limitations, or to avoid some redundancy in the nature of the experience shared.

Some poets are represented through several poems: Dickinson, Frost, Longfellow, Donne. I debated whether that was wise and soon decided that a poet should *not* be penalized simply because his or her work is as ingrained in our literary and historical awareness as the work of these poets. In addition, it is interesting to see how great poetry drops barriers, how the same poet speaks personally, even intimately, to very different readers. To take Dickinson, for example, the anthology has five of her poems with five corresponding essays. The readers are a U.S. senator, a college professor, a Methodist minister, a twelve-year old 7th grader, and a retired teacher. This range is further evidence of the word's power to suggest, rather than define.

❧❧❧

And now it is time to "say grace," for I must spread abundant gratitude around. I am grateful to the readers who shared so generously of their experiences, so that we might celebrate the encounter that is poetry. Some of these readers have well-known names; others are well known only in the more intimate circles of their lives. Either way, these contributors took time out of full schedules to ponder about poetry and to share something of value with the rest of us.

I am grateful to the poets or their estates, publishers, and agents, for allowing the use of their work, much of it not in the public domain, as you will see from the acknowledgments section. In many cases, authors and publishers kindly reduced their usual reprint fees; a few waived their fees entirely.

I am grateful to the Poetry Society of Virginia and the Virginia Writers Club. The statewide membership of these organizations provided exceptional support for this project in numerous ways. Among other things, the PSV and the VWC ensured that my call for submissions reached libraries, learning institutions, writers' groups, and literary clubs across the Commonwealth. Without their efforts, this anthology would never have come to be.

I am grateful to Linda Layne, owner of Cedar Creek Publishing. Her belief in this project, from its inception, have given me the kind of support only a publisher can provide, whenever it was needed. I could not ask for more.

Most importantly, I am grateful, more than words can express (but then again, he knows all the words I ever say) to Bill Starnes, my husband, without whose love and tangible sustenance this project—and many of my activities as Poet Laureate—would not have been possible.

> Sofia M. Starnes
> Poet Laureate of Virginia, 2012-1014
> Williamsburg, Virginia

Beauty

I imagine the two of them
sitting in a garden
among late-blossoming roses
and dark cascades of leaves...

Lisel Mueller, the poet

Quite simply, they loved each other.
That is enough to know.
The myriad forms of love
are a beautiful mystery.

JoAnn Falletta, the reader

Why Then Do We Not Despair

Anna Akhmatova,
Translated by Stanley Kunitz and Max Hayward

Everything is plundered, betrayed, sold,
Death's great black wing scrapes the air,
Misery gnaws to the bone.
Why then do we not despair?

By day, from the surrounding woods,
cherries blow summer into town;
at night the deep transparent skies
glitter with new galaxies.

And the miraculous comes so close
to the ruined, dirty houses—
something not known to anyone at all,
but wild in our breast for centuries.

Sharron Singleton, of Scottsville, writes:

Anna Akhmatova is regarded as one of the great Russian poets. Her life and writing played out against the transition from pre-Revolutionary Russia to the cataclysmic Russian revolution and Soviet rule, and she was frequently confronted with governmental opposition to her work. Yet she was deeply loved by the Russian people, in part because she did not abandon her country during difficult political times.

One of the common denominators of great poetry and one of the reasons why this poem is close to my heart is that, no matter when it was written, it seems ageless and speaks in a contemporary and universal language. While this poem was written in 1921 in the chaotic aftermath of the Russian revolution, it could have been written today, as our entire planet and its inhabitants are so often plundered and betrayed by greed and the seekers of power. Yet in spite of human-caused ruin and waste, this poem asserts that the natural world continues to be restorative and creative, to bestow its blessings, as its compelling metaphors and startling clarity of language declare that, "cherries blow summer into town" and "skies/ glitter with new galaxies." How can one not love a poem which claims in such a stunning way that, in spite of everything, deep within the human spirit is the potential for newness of life, hope rising from the ashes —which claims that that which is simply human is at the same time miraculous, "wild in our breast for centuries."

Kubla Khan

Or a Vision in a Dream. A Fragment.

Samuel Taylor Coleridge

In Xanadu did Kubla Khan
A stately pleasure-dome decree:
Where Alph, the sacred river, ran
Through caverns measureless to man
Down to a sunless sea.
So twice five miles of fertile ground
With walls and towers were girdled round;
And there were gardens bright with sinuous rills,
Where blossomed many an incense-bearing tree;
And here were forests ancient as the hills,
Enfolding sunny spots of greenery.

But oh! that deep romantic chasm which slanted
Down the green hill athwart a cedarn cover!
A savage place! as holy and enchanted
As e'er beneath a waning moon was haunted
By woman wailing for her demon-lover!
And from this chasm, with ceaseless turmoil seething,
As if this earth in fast thick pants were breathing,
A mighty fountain momently was forced:
Amid whose swift half-intermitted burst
Huge fragments vaulted like rebounding hail,
Or chaffy grain beneath the thresher's flail:
And 'mid these dancing rocks at once and ever
It flung up momently the sacred river.
Five miles meandering with a mazy motion
Through wood and dale the sacred river ran,
Then reached the caverns measureless to man,
And sank in tumult to a lifeless ocean;

And 'mid this tumult Kubla heard from far
Ancestral voices prophesying war!
The shadow of the dome of pleasure
Floated midway on the waves;
Where was heard the mingled measure
From the fountain and the caves.
It was a miracle of rare device,
A sunny pleasure-dome with caves of ice!

A damsel with a dulcimer
In a vision once I saw:
It was an Abyssinian maid
And on her dulcimer she played,
Singing of Mount Abora.
Could I revive within me
Her symphony and song,
To such a deep delight 'twould win me,
That with music loud and long,
I would build that dome in air,
That sunny dome! those caves of ice!
And all who heard should see them there,
And all should cry, Beware! Beware!
His flashing eyes, his floating hair!
Weave a circle round him thrice,
And close your eyes with holy dread
For he on honey-dew hath fed,
And drunk the milk of Paradise.

Maggie Pecsok, of Virginia Beach, writes:

When I first read "Kubla Khan," I wrote it off as a jumble of pompous and incoherent words. Frankly, I found it obnoxious; Coleridge was just rubbing it in that my vocabulary needed improvement. Then Dr. Kidd, my junior English teacher and mentor, professed it was his favorite poem. "Typical English teacher," I scoffed. My disdain only softened when I participated in the Poetry Out Loud competition, a nationwide poetry recitation contest.

Discussing poetry with a mentor opened my eyes; talking with Dr. Kidd made me feel as if I were in a French salon during the Enlightenment, and I grew determined to understand Coleridge's poem. To my surprise, untangling "Kubla Khan" proved to be as much fun as physics homework. I realized (slightly grudgingly) how closed-minded I had been; poetry holds the same aspect of discovery I so adore in the sciences. Behind the stanzas I found the portrait of a troubled genius. I found music in the cadence of the words. I found my favorite poem.

To me, "Kubla Khan" represents the power of positivity. When I let go of my negative preconceptions, I was able not just to understand the poem, but also to appreciate its complexity as a promise of eternal discovery. Because I memorized it for the competition, I carry it with me wherever I go—as a constant reminder that everything offers the opportunity for joy as long as I am willing to look.

Moon

Billy Collins

The moon is full tonight
an illustration for sheet music,
an image in Matthew Arnold
glimmering on the English Channel,
or a ghost over a smoldering battlefield
in one of the history plays.

It's as full as it was
in that poem by Coleridge
where he carries his year-old son
into the orchard behind the cottage
and turns the baby's face to the sky
to see for the first time
the earth's bright companion,
something amazing to make his crying seem small.

And if you wanted to follow this example,
tonight would be the night
to carry some tiny creature outside
and introduce him to the moon.

And if your house has no child,
you can always gather into your arms
the sleeping infant of yourself,
as I have done tonight,
and carry him outdoors,
all limp in his tattered blanket,
making sure to steady his lolling head
with the palm of your hand.

And while the wind ruffles the pear trees
in the corner of the orchard
and dark roses wave against a stone wall,
you can turn him on your shoulder
and walk in circles on the lawn
drunk with the light.
You can lift him up into the sky,
your eyes nearly as wide as his,
as the moon climbs high into the night.

ക്ക്ക

Angela Anselmo, of James City County, writes:

I have always loved the moon. In childhood it seemed to me like a toy I couldn't touch but could enjoy, as it changed from a silver sliver to a perfect circle of light in the sky. Throughout my lifetime my fascination with the moon has not diminished. Although man has walked on its surface and given us proof of its substance, to me it remains a magical and mystical vision. In "Moon" Billy Collins enhances that vision with images of the moon "glimmering on the English Channel" or "a ghost over a smoldering battlefield." I am reminded of the timeless and universal inspiration the moon has been for poets.

My response to Billy Collins's "Moon" goes much deeper than being enthralled by its lovely images, however. It is the poet's surprise transition from simply introducing a child to the beauty of the full moon, to the words "gather into your arms/ the sleeping infant of yourself,/ as I have done tonight,/ and carry him outdoors," that I find so awesome. How wonderful to discover, in these words, such a poetic and elemental suggestion, one that allows me to revive the wonder of childhood and restore my dormant or "sleeping" youthful self; to, temporarily at least, find comfort in becoming my own child and treating myself lovingly to the magic of the moon and other wonders of nature.

My River runs to thee

Emily Dickinson

My River runs to thee –
Blue Sea! Wilt welcome me?
My River waits reply –
Oh Sea – look graciously –
I'll fetch thee Brooks
From spotted nooks –
Say – Sea – Take *Me*!

Rachel Brandon, of Leesburg, writes:

"My River runs to thee" reminds me of how beautiful and powerful nature is. This poem talks about how a river is asking the ocean for acceptance. It really captures the image of a flowing stream pleading to the ocean to be received. The force and the beauty of nature always capture my interest.

This poem felt nearest to me because I consider myself a nature girl. I've grown up visiting the beach every summer, and I like being outside. I enjoy fishing, boating, and many activities that revolve around water. I also enjoy hiking in the mountains near streams and waterfalls. When I am close to the water, I feel at peace.

I researched Emily Dickinson's life a little bit, and I learned that she wrote a lot about nature and death. In this poem I think she was trying to capture the image of nature, while really talking about herself, how she was asking the world for acceptance. She was probably imagining the kind of peace I feel when I am around water.

These are the days when Birds come back

Emily Dickinson

These are the days when Birds come back –
A very few – a Bird or two –
To take a backward look.

These are the days when skies resume
The old – old sophistries of June –
A blue and gold mistake.

Oh fraud that cannot cheat the Bee –
Almost thy plausibility
Induces my belief.

Till ranks of seeds their witness bear –
And softly thro' the altered air
Hurries a timid leaf.

Oh Sacrament of summer days,
Oh Last Communion in the Haze –
Permit a child to join.

Thy sacred emblems to partake –
Thy consecrated bread to take
And thine immortal wine!

Marguerite Thoburn Watkins, of Lynchburg, writes:

After a childhood in India and boarding school in the foothills of the Himalayas, and after a career teaching handicapped children in Lynchburg, Virginia, I find myself living at Westminster-Canterbury, a retirement community near the Blue Ridge Mountains, and working on memoir, completing the circle of my life.

I knew I would choose one of Emily Dickinson's poems as my nearest poem—but which one? I like so many so much, yet I keep returning to "These are the days...." It has become my favorite, although I do not quite know why—perhaps because of the move from a celebration of summer's beauty to that of sacrament, the spiritual realm; perhaps because to Emily Dickinson, nature and sacrament are the same. And I like a poem that starts in one place and leads the reader somewhere else: always a gentle surprise, the way Emily does it. She poured passion and longing into her unconventional poetry.

How sad that she had to write without recognition during her lifetime! Or maybe the sadness is ours, and not hers. After all, she certainly retained her persistence and sense of fun. I resonate with that.

Each and All

Ralph Waldo Emerson

Little thinks, in the field, yon red-cloaked clown,
Of thee, from the hill-top looking down;
And the heifer, that lows in the upland farm,
Far-heard, lows not thine ear to charm;
The sexton tolling the bell at noon,
Dreams not that great Napoleon
Stops his horse, and lists with delight,
Whilst his files sweep round yon Alpine height;
Nor knowest thou what argument
Thy life to thy neighbor's creed has lent:
All are needed by each one,
Nothing is fair or good alone.

I thought the sparrow's note from heaven,
Singing at dawn on the alder bough;
I brought him home in his nest at even;—
He sings the song, but it pleases not now;
For I did not bring home the river and sky;
He sang to my ear; they sang to my eye.

The delicate shells lay on the shore;
The bubbles of the latest wave
Fresh pearls to their enamel gave;
And the bellowing of the savage sea
Greeted their safe escape to me;
I wiped away the weeds and foam,
And fetched my sea-born treasures home;
But the poor, unsightly, noisome things
Had left their beauty on the shore
With the sun, and the sand, and the wild uproar.

The lover watched his graceful maid
As 'mid the virgin train she strayed,
Nor knew her beauty's best attire
Was woven still by the snow-white quire;
At last she came to his hermitage,
Like the bird from the woodlands to the cage,—
The gay enchantment was undone,
A gentle wife, but fairy none.

Then I said, "I covet Truth;
Beauty is unripe childhood's cheat,—
I leave it behind with the games of youth."
As I spoke, beneath my feet
The ground-pine curled its pretty wreath,
Running over the club-moss burrs;
I inhaled the violet's breath;
Around me stood the oaks and firs;
Pine cones and acorns lay on the ground;
Above me soared the eternal sky,
Full of light and deity;
Again I saw, again I heard,
The rolling river, the morning bird;—
Beauty through my senses stole,
I yielded myself to the perfect whole.

Stuart C. Nottingham, of Alexandria, writes:

I first encountered my nearest poem "Each and All" by Ralph Waldo Emerson in the Assistant Principal's office of Granby High School in 1947. Mr. Harrell had disapproved of my playing solitaire in study hall. He took me to his office and made me read this poem. It was his way of teaching me that I am not alone in this world, that my behavior may have influence on others that I never intended. These lines are direct to Mr. Harrell's lesson:

> Nor knowest thou what argument
> Thy life to thy neighbor's creed has lent:

The poem continues with several examples of how each is a part of a larger whole. The most beautiful are these lines:

> I thought the sparrow's note from heaven,
> Singing at dawn on the alder bough;
> I brought him home in his nest at even;—
> He sings the song, but it pleases not now;
> For I did not bring home the river and sky;
> He sang to my ear; they sang to my eye.

The sparrow's song alone does not deliver the whole experience. You must have the alder bough, the river, and the sky. The whole is necessary. "I yielded myself to the perfect whole" is the last line of the poem. Each time I read the poem I get closer to accepting myself as a part of a greater whole. And so, this poem continues to impart its lessons to me and my children, grandchildren, and great-grandchildren, all of whom have received a copy.

A Winter Light

John Haines

We still go about our lives
in shadow, pouring the white cup full
with a hand half in darkness.

Paring potatoes, our heads
vent over a dream—
glazed window through which
the long, yellow sundown looks.

By candle or firelight
your face still holds
a mystery that once
filled caves with the color
of unforgettable beasts.

Carey K. Bagdassarian, of Williamsburg, writes:

John Haines lived from the hard land in the Alaskan wilderness. Hunting, fishing, and trapping to survive, he grew slowly in knowledge over the years, learning from his own mistakes and from talking to the few old men still making a go of it. His attention to animal footprints, river melt, to wind and snowdrift, was necessarily drastic. I suspect Haines wanted to understand what it meant to live close to human origins, and he wrestled in his poetry with the contradictions inherent in this experience.

But I'm also struck by a strange paradoxical softness in him, a soft sort of paying attention. When I waterproof my leather hiking boots, carefully working oils and waxes into them, I have, if I'm paying soft attention, John Haines and his poetry with me. Sometimes, when I remember to, I work by candle-light, waiting for those unforgettable beasts that might come only in that quiet. And when my own heart is less iron and I'm lucky, I sense the stories that still circle our origins and call like the owls John Haines loved.

God's Grandeur

Gerard Manley Hopkins

The world is charged with the grandeur of God.
    It will flame out, like shining from shook foil;
    It gathers to a greatness, like the ooze of oil
Crushed. Why do men then now not reck his rod?
Generations have trod, have trod, have trod;
    And all is seared with trade; bleared, smeared with toil;
    And wears man's smudge and shares man's smell: the soil
Is bare now, nor can foot feel, being shod.

And for all this, nature is never spent;
    There lives the dearest freshness deep down things;
And though the last lights off the black West went
    Oh, morning, at the brown brink eastward, springs—
Because the Holy Ghost over the bent
    World broods with warm breast and with ah! bright wings.

David Partie, of Lynchburg, writes:

Of all the poems that I have read, "God's Grandeur" best captures the sense of the sacred, the presence of God permeating the world. It affirms that the world is fallen, bearing the stamp of man who has marred it but not destroyed it. The world is bent, but not irrevocably broken, marked with "man's smudge" but not mangled beyond repair. The stamp of the original created world can still be perceived, but its stirrings, its freshness are "deep down" so that we have to look carefully to find them.

I love the exclamation "ah!" near the end of the poem's last line. To me it is an "ah" of delighted surprise, of recognition, of discovery, of reverence for the Creator, even of worship. That "ah" points to the mystery of the invisible Spirit brooding over "the bent/ World," as a mother hen broods over a nest of eggs or as the Spirit before the dawn of creation brooded over empty, shapeless water.

The world is certainly marred with violence, cruelty, selfishness, and greed. Nature and man undergo the same cycle of birth, growth, decay, and death. But the sense of the sacred and the promise of renewal are still there for us to celebrate. I try to look for God's grandeur in what He has created just beyond my doorstep when I pick up the morning newspaper. I try to open my sleep-filled eyes wider so that I can see the "dearest freshness deep down things" that sometimes lies (ah!) just below the surface.

Heft

Richard Jones

I hold the words *broken bones*
in my hand; I hold the words
rib cage, the word *heart.*
I lift every word
like a stone or a feather.

The more beautiful words,
like *heaven*, or *nothingness*,
feel exactly the same
as *fence post* or *mailbox*,
lamplight or *shoelace.*

Spirit
flits like a tongue of flame,
as insubstantial in the hand
as its brother, *death*,
which weighs exactly the same as *life.*

Vivian Teter, of Norfolk, writes:

We are blessed in our lives when we are companioned by a poem that finds us (or returns to us) at an exact moment of our need. Such is the case for me with Richard Jones's "Heft." I taught the book in which this poem appears, APROPOS OF NOTHING, in my contemporary poetry course, and then, in life's bustle, tucked it away like a beautiful strand of pearls whose luster and curve I admired.

Then the unthinkable happened: a younger sister stricken with brain cancer; a journey of caretaking begun. One night, shivering in fear, facing the word incurable, I found in my bed-stand drawer Richard's book and opened it to "Heft," its every word anchored in space, its voice an old friend still near. And the poem's beauty bore truth: in the hand, "Spirit" and "heaven" have as much heft, as fair a chance, as "nothingness" and "shoelace." The word terminal weighed no more than the word love. Fed by poetry's gift, I could feed my sister.

And for everyday living past crises, this poem's wisdom and music ring true. We often hold tight to words, repeating them for pleasure or comfort or to savor the mystery they body forth, like the mystery of "Spirit" as "insubstantial in the hand/ as its brother, death." And the mystery of "heaven" counterpointing "nothingness." For me, "Heft" enacts the very mystery of our world's balance of beginnings and endings, joys and sorrows. And in times of great need, words in such poems braid, line by line, a firm, taut rope as we edge along life's precipices, holding in our hands both "broken bones" and "lamplight."

When Earth's Last Picture Is Painted

Rudyard Kipling

When Earth's last picture is painted
    And the tubes are twisted and dried,
When the oldest colors have faded,
    And the youngest critic has died,
We shall rest, and faith, we shall need it—
    Lie down for an aeon or two,
'Till The Master of All Good Workmen
    Shall put us to work anew.

And those that were good shall be happy;
    They shall sit in a golden chair;
They shall splash at a ten league canvas
    With brushes of comet's hair.
They shall find real saints to draw from—
    Magdalene, Peter, and Paul;
They shall work for an age at a sitting
    And never be tired at all!

And only The Master shall praise us,
    And only The Master shall blame;
And no one shall work for money,
    And no one shall work for fame,
But each for the joy of the working,
    And each, in his separate star,
Shall draw the Thing as he sees It
    For the God of Things as They are!

❧❧❧

Al C. Bradley, of Abingdon, writes:

"When Earth's Last Picture is Painted" is a poem that my mother Gilley Bradley learned in an English class at Welch High School in Welch, West Virginia. She remembered this poem all her life and would share it with others as the occasion permitted. On one such occasion, well into her eighties and having survived brain surgery for a meningioma, Gilley presented a program for her Circle (Clara Tucker Perry Circle) at Abingdon United Methodist Church. The program included her favorite hymns and this favorite poem.

Gilley was able to cook, clean (she preferred cooking!), drive, shop, visit until her 89th year, at which time she fell in her entryway at home and hit her head, an accident that resulted in a cerebral hemorrhage. In true "Gilley" fashion, she survived this injury, but she did lose her short-term memory. Even so, I remember her reciting this poem at her 90th birthday party, held in her home, in Abingdon, to the amazement of many of her friends.

Mother died in 2004 at the age of ninety-four, and her granddaughter Renee Ringley Taylor read this poem at her funeral. Many folks requested copies of it; I know that whenever they read the poem they will think of Gilley.

Thoughtless Cruelty

Charles Lamb

There, Robert, you have kill'd that fly,—
And should you thousand ages try
The life you've taken to supply,
   You could not do it.

You surely must have been devoid
Of thought and sense, to have destroy'd
A thing which no way you annoy'd—
   You'll one day rue it.

'Twas but a fly perhaps you'll say,
That's born in April, dies in May;
That does but just learn to display
   His wings one minute,

And in the next is vanish'd quite.
A bird devours it in his flight—
Or come a cold blast in the night,
   There's no breath in it.

The bird but seeks his proper food—
And Providence, whose power endu'd
That fly with life, when it thinks good,
   May justly take it.

But you have no excuses for't—
A life by Nature made so short,
Less reason is that you for sport
   Should shorter make it.

A fly a little thing you rate—
But, Robert do not estimate
A creature's pain by small or great;
   The greatest being

Can have but fibres, nerves, and flesh,
And these the smallest ones possess,
Although their frame and structure less
   Escape our seeing.

Arooba Ayaz, of Virginia Beach, writes:

Art is truly one of the most powerful things on earth; it always makes us think and helps deepen our understanding of our world and each other. I enjoy many types of art myself; I like to draw, paint, and write. The centuries-old art of poetry is one of my favorites.

The beauty behind Charles Lamb's poem "Thoughtless Cruelty" is that it makes us think by using a simple analogy, that of merely swatting a fly. Such a small thing! Yet, it manages to reawaken our humanity, not through lecturing or in a homily, but in a rather conversational tone.

As an adolescent, I have a tendency to tune out lectures. In this case, although the poem was written over a century ago, its casual tone made it very relatable to me—and the first thing the poem made me feel was guilt. We all have a Robert inside of us, as well as a conscience. Lamb not only gets us to feel remorse for merely killing a fly, but his poem also nudges our consciences further. When I read the poem, and then recited it at the Poetry Out Loud competition, I felt all of the Robert inside me diminish, along with every one of Robert's excuses, which Lamb refutes. The old but universal message of respect that Lamb wanted to share with us became blatantly obvious. Through the art of poetry, he expressed a problem that was present in his time. After reading his poem, I realize that the problem is still present today. The poem made me think, as all great art should.

Dust

Dorianne Laux

Someone spoke to me last night,
told me the truth. Just a few words,
but I recognized it.
I knew I should make myself get up,
write it down, but it was late,
and I was exhausted from working
all day in the garden, moving rocks.
Now, I remember only the flavor—
not like food, sweet or sharp.
More like a fine powder, like dust.
And I wasn't elated or frightened,
but simply rapt, aware.
That's how it is sometimes—
God comes to your window,
all bright light and black wings,
and you're just too tired to open it.

Cameron Conaway, of Charlottesville, writes:

My sharpest moments of poetic inspiration come in the few minutes of mindfulness that dangle near the edge of sleep. "Dust" by Dorianne Laux contains, in a few crisp lines, the insights into my creative method that I'd sought unsuccessfully for years.

It's not every night, maybe a few nights per month (if I'm lucky) that inspiration comes. When it does, I experience it as creativity in its purest form—and as nothing at all. Nothing, that is, until it intersects with the will. I know "I should make myself get up,/ write it down," but few things can weigh the will down as heavily as exhaustion. In the morning and sometimes all throughout the week, I'll carry my notebook around in an attempt to track down the creativity I was "just too tired to open." I'll get a fragment at the dojo, maybe a bit while in the woods or while waiting in line at the post office. None of it feels full, distinct. It's not the food but the "fine powder, like dust," infinitesimal specks of something that can only be made whole through the seemingly impossible task of finding the other parts. The "flavor" is both reminder and tease; it is "all bright light and black wings." It is evidence that creativity cannot land unless accepted.

The Owl and the Pussy-Cat

Edward Lear

The Owl and the Pussy-Cat went to sea
In a beautiful pea-green boat,
They took some honey, and plenty of money,
Wrapped up in a five-pound note.
The Owl looked up to the stars above,
And sang to a small guitar,
"O lovely Pussy! O Pussy, my love,
What a beautiful Pussy you are,
          You are,
          You are!
What a beautiful Pussy you are!"

Pussy said to the Owl, "You elegant fowl!
How charmingly sweet you sing!
O let us be married! too long we have tarried:
But what shall we do for a ring?"
They sailed away for a year and a day,
To the land where the Bong-tree grows,
And there in a wood a Piggy-wig stood,
With a ring at the end of his nose,
          His nose,
          His nose,
With a ring at the end of his nose.

"Dear Pig, are you willing to sell for one shilling
Your ring?" Said the Piggy, "I will."
So they took it away, and were married next day
By the Turkey who lives on the hill.

They dined on mince, and slices of quince,
Which they ate with a runcible spoon;
And hand in hand, on the edge of the sand,
They danced by the light of the moon,
　　The moon,
　　The moon,
They danced by the light of the moon.

≼≼≼

**"Grandma" Mary Jean Kledzik, of Norfolk, with
Graham West Thomas, 4 years old, of Carrollton, writes:**

This poem is Graham's favorite. It is also an old favorite of mine, from when I was six years old and received the book I read it from today, turning the same pages. It takes me to the heart of romance and love. I delight in the musicality, rhythm, rhyming, and fantasy. Or, as Graham quite simply puts it, "It makes me feel happy. I love it!"

Evangeline

(an excerpt)

Henry Wadsworth Longfellow

Somewhat apart from the village,
    and nearer the Basin of Minas,
Benedict Bellefontaine,
    the wealthiest farmer of Grand-Pré,
Dwelt on his goodly acres;
    and with him, directing his household,
Gentle Evangeline lived,
    his child, and the pride of the village.
Stalworth and stately in form
    was the man of seventy winters;
Hearty and hale was he,
    an oak that is covered with snowflakes;
White as the snow were his locks,
    and his cheeks as brown as the oak-leaves.
Fair was she to behold,
    that maiden of seventeen summers.
Black were her eyes as the berry
    that grows on the thorn by the wayside,
Black, yet how softly they gleamed
    beneath the brown shade of her tresses!
Sweet was her breath as the breath
    of kine that feed in the meadows.
When in the harvest heat
    she bore to the reapers at noontide
Flagons of home-brewed ale,
    ah! fair in sooth was the maiden.
Fairer was she when, on Sunday morn,
    while the bell from its turret
Sprinkled with holy sounds the air,
    as the priest with his hyssop
Sprinkles the congregation,
    and scatters blessings upon them,
Down the long street she passed,
    with her chaplet of beads and her missal,

Wearing her Norman cap,
    and her kirtle of blue, and the ear-rings,
Brought in the olden time from France,
    and since, as an heirloom,
Handed down from mother to child,
    through long generations.
But a celestial brightness—
    a more ethereal beauty—
Shone on her face and encircled her form,
    when, after confession,
Homeward serenely she walked
    with God's benediction upon her.
When she had passed, it seemed
    like the ceasing of exquisite music.

∾∾∾

Tucker Withers, of Aldie, writes:

I'm not sure at what age I first read "Evangeline." Maybe I was eleven or twelve when the visions of Nova Scotia's Annapolis Valley and Louisiana's St. Martinville came into my mind. Not only did "Evangeline," written in 1847, inspire me to visit these faraway places, but the poem also inspired America and Canada in many ways. Starting in the 1850s, lithographers published hand-colored prints of Evangeline. Currier & Ives led the way with at least five different versions. Statues of a sad Evangeline were erected, a movie was made in the 1920s, and there is a line of Evangeline food products.

I have collected many Evangeline items over the years, but my favorite is a Currier & Ives finely colored large folio, from 1864, titled "The Home of Evangeline." I purchased it twenty-five years ago in New York, not far from where it was painted. It depicts Evangeline and her father, Benedict Bellefontaine, a wealthy farmer, sitting on the porch of their substantial oak house with the village of Grand Pré behind them. As is typical with many of the lithographs, several lines of the poem appear underneath the title.

Although the characters are fictional, some scholars believe Longfellow based them on real-life people. And the story is true. The English expelled the French from Nova Scotia in 1755, and these Acadians were forced to settle in America's southland, with many living in Louisiana near the Bayou Teche.

Starting in my early twenties, I made pilgrimages to all areas connected with Evangeline, from the trail that now bears her name through the Annapolis Valley in Nova Scotia to her fictitious grave in St. Martinville, Louisiana. There is a myriad of historical markers which tell the tragic Acadian story. Now married with children, I have taken my family to retrace my footsteps and the footsteps of Evangeline.

The Village Blacksmith

Henry Wadsworth Longfellow

Under a spreading chestnut-tree
The village smithy stands;
The smith, a mighty man is he,
With large and sinewy hands;
And the muscles of his brawny arms
Are strong as iron bands.

His hair is crisp, and black, and long,
His face is like the tan;
His brow is wet with honest sweat,
He earns whate'er he can,
And looks the whole world in the face,
For he owes not any man.

Week in, week out, from morn till night,
You can hear his bellows blow;
You can hear him swing his heavy sledge,
With measured beat and slow,
Like a sexton ringing the village bell,
When the evening sun is low.

And children coming home from school
Look in at the open door;
They love to see the flaming forge,
And hear the bellows roar,
And catch the burning sparks that fly
Like chaff from a threshing floor.

He goes on Sunday to the church,
And sits among his boys;
He hears the parson pray and preach,
He hears his daughter's voice,
Singing in the village choir,
And it makes his heart rejoice.

It sounds to him like her mother's voice,
Singing in Paradise!
He needs must think of her once more,
How in the grave she lies;
And with his hard, rough hand he wipes
A tear out of his eyes.

Toiling,—rejoicing,—sorrowing,
Onward through life he goes;
Each morning sees some task begin,
Each evening sees it close;
Something attempted, something done,
He earned a night's repose.

Thanks, thanks to thee, my worthy friend,
For the lesson thou has taught!
Thus at the flaming forge of life
Our fortunes must be wrought;
Thus on its sound anvil shaped
Each burning deed and thought.

Linda Nash, of Fairfax, writes:

"The Village Blacksmith" brings back memories of growing up in the 1960s. My family was engaged in conversation over dinner one evening when my father began to recite "The Village Blacksmith." He then looked at us and announced that he would give each child a quarter if we also would memorize the poem. Well, I was never even enticed. A quarter! Why bother! Yet now I would pay my father handsomely for sparking the germ of poetry in my soul. I learned that he had spent his own young years listening to his siblings and parents around the dinner table recite poetry. The poems made him look beyond the facts of life and dramatically invoke a higher calling.

In "The Village Blacksmith" I see the strength to live life fully. The blacksmith embodies America: "His brow is wet with honest sweat,/ he earns whate'er he can,/ and looks the whole world in the face,/ for he owes not any man." There is something about this man's honesty, his cleanness and his "forging" in the fire that I find incredibly enthralling. And I wonder: does anyone desire to be honest anymore, as he desired it? And that resonating rhyme! How I loved and love to hear it!

It will take a poet to turn the hearts of men from death to life in its fullness. I am forever grateful to my father for opening my eyes—and ears—to that. For my part, as a singer/songwriter, I will never stop chanting, as in the Song of Solomon: "Arise, my love, and come away...."

Sea Fever

John Masefield

I must go down to the seas again, to the lonely sea and the sky,
And all I ask is a tall ship and a star to steer her by;
And the wheel's kick and the wind's song and the white sail's shaking,
And a grey mist on the sea's face, and a grey dawn breaking,

I must go down to the seas again, for the call of the running tide
Is a wild call and a clear call that may not be denied;
And all I ask is a windy day with the white clouds flying,
And the flung spray and the blown spume, and the sea-gulls crying.

I must go down to the seas again, to the vagrant gypsy life,
To the gull's way and the whale's way where the wind's like a whetted knife;
And all I ask is a merry yarn from a laughing fellow-rover,
And quiet sleep and a sweet dream when the long trick's over.

֍֍֍

Martha W. Steger, of Midlothian, writes:

I found the version of "Sea Fever" featured here on an internet website, yet my earliest hearing of the poem was a recitation by my father when I was in the third or fourth grade in Parksley on Virginia's Eastern Shore. He read the first line without the word "go," which was what Masefield had originally written and hated to change because the addition altered the poem's rhythm. This poem had great meaning for my father because he, like my brother and I, had grown up on the tiny peninsula between the Atlantic Ocean and the Chesapeake Bay; his father had been a waterman and farmer.

Before my father's explanation of the poem's change, I'd assumed the words of printed literature, once written, were set in stone; learning they sometimes change from one draft to the next gave me insight into poetry as living and breathing—an organic thing.

I'd written stories about children in notebooks since I was six years old, but I never dreamed that writing would become my life's work (primarily journalistic and public-relations writing, but also essays, magazine articles, short stories, and, yes, a few published poems…). Knowing a piece of work can change—like "the wheel's kick and the wind's song" in the poem—has always been comforting.

Harvest

Jim Wayne Miller

Now his whole life seemed weathered and old-fashioned.
When others spoke, their words made pictures
With gleaming surfaces and metal trim.
He spoke drafty pole barns and garden plots.
His customs had a mustiness, a smokehouse mold
About them; his shriveled wisdom hung like peppers
And shuckybeans from a cabin rafter.
Beliefs leaned back like doors with broken hinges,
Stood sunken like a rotten springhouse roof.

Still, he thought of songs landlocked two hundred
Years, living in coves and hollers, far from
Home, by creeks and waterfalls, and springdrain
Trickles,—songs that still remembered the salt salt sea
And held all past time green in the month of May
And made all love and death and sorrow sweet.

So he wasn't sad to see his life gathered
Up in books, kept on a shelf like dry seeds
In an envelope, or carried far off
Like Spanish needles in a fox's fur.
His people brought the salt sea in their songs;
Now they moved mountains to the cities
And made all love and death and sorrow sweet there.

Heaviness was always left behind
To perish, to topple like a stone chimney

But what was lightest lasted, live in song.

৵৵৵

Rita Sims Quillen, of Gate City, writes:

Like most young, aspiring poets, I thought poems had to be about Subjects Of Cosmic Importance: love and death and the "meaning of life"! So, I wrote mostly horrible, incoherent poetry that didn't accomplish anything. I did have a few more concrete, vivid poems that I had written about my husband's grandmother, an amazing woman, full of stories and wisdom, and the most naturally lyrical conversationalist I'd ever met. I took the poems about her, as well as the works I later came to call the "labyrinth of abstraction poems," to one of my college professors. He kindly made no comment on the latter poems, but said of the grandmother poems, "These are wonderful. Your writing reminds me of Fred Chappell."

I had never heard of Chappell at that point, but filled with pride, I rushed straight to the library in search of his poetry and found two poetry chapbooks. (They would later comprise Chappell's work, MIDQUEST, one of the great collections in American literature.)

Time stopped in that library that afternoon. I read the chapbooks cover-to-cover twice. Then I began to look at poetry shelved next to his. There was a book by a man named Jim Wayne Miller and another by a mountain man with three names—Jeff Daniel Marion. I devoured these books. Late that evening, I left the library a changed person, a changed writer.

What I learned that day from these writers is that I could write about my everyday world—life, family, culture, and traditions—and produce art. Chappell, Miller, and Marion were writing about their history here, in the Appalachian Mountains. I could write about barns and gardens and making apple butter, and in doing so, I would be covering all those Subjects Of Cosmic Importance. Miller's poem "Harvest" captures beautifully the revelation I had on that long-ago afternoon.

Lines and Squares

A. A. Milne

Whenever I walk in a London street,
I'm ever so careful to watch my feet;
And I keep in the squares,
And the masses of bears,
Who wait at the corners all ready to eat
The sillies who tread on the lines of the street
Go back to their lairs,
And I say to them, "Bears,
Just look how I'm walking in all the squares!"

And the little bears growl to each other, "He's mine,
As soon as he's silly and steps on a line."
And some of the bigger bears try to pretend
That they came round the corner to look for a friend;
And they try to pretend that nobody cares
Whether you walk on the lines or squares.
But only the sillies believe their talk;
It's ever so portant how you walk.
And it's ever so jolly to call out, "Bears,
Just watch me walking in all the squares!"

Kathi Mestayer, of James City County, writes:

When asked what my nearest poem was, I immediately thought of A. A. Milne. I had his children's poetry books WHEN WE WERE VERY YOUNG and NOW WE ARE SIX since childhood, and actually prefer the poems to his Winnie-the-Pooh stories, which are much better known.

Two of my favorite poems are "King John's Christmas" and this one, "Lines and Squares," which I have had memorized for a really, really long time — at least twenty years! — and which I recite to myself when the mood strikes me — or just to make sure I don't forget it.

I like the "imaginary" bears (but how do we really know?), the child's fearlessness, and his absolute, proud rebelliousness. And the word, "portant!"

Romantics

Johannes Brahms and Clara Schumann

Lisel Mueller

The modern biographers worry
"how far it went," their tender friendship.
They wonder just what it means
when he writes he thinks of her constantly,
his guardian angel, beloved friend.
The modern biographers ask
the rude, irrelevant question
of our age, as if the event
of two bodies meshing together
establishes the degree of love,
forgetting how softly Eros walked
in the nineteenth century, how a hand
held overlong or a gaze anchored
in someone's eyes could unseat a heart,
and nuances of address not known
in our egalitarian language
could make the redolent air
tremble and shimmer with the heat
of possibility. Each time I hear
the Intermezzi, sad
and lavish in their tenderness,
I imagine the two of them
sitting in a garden
among late-blossoming roses
and dark cascades of leaves,
letting the landscape speak for them,
leaving us nothing to overhear.

JoAnn Falletta, of Norfolk, writes:

This poem has great meaning for me, not only because I love the music of these two great artists, but also because of the gentle and profound portrait of love it presents.

I had always wondered about the "exact" nature of the relationship between Brahms and Clara, and reading this fragrant and shimmering poem, I realized that it did not matter. Quite simply, they loved each other. That is enough to know. The myriad forms of love are a beautiful mystery.

Another Poem Beginning with a
Line from Nina Cassian

Giavanna Munafo

I'm getting lovelier by the hour, and the intricacies
of my skin increase as I speak. Each hand alone
tells the stories of decades, of a woman who has lived.

Long ago, I tell you, I made use of myself, weeding
a neighbor's garden. Each day after school I plucked
and sorted, tramped and thinned the fragrant shoots.

I snatched up weeds with one hand and pinched back
basil gone to flower with the other, delivering zucchini
and tomatoes, a few melons, just before dark.

Not long after, I spent a season with the orphans.
I was young, mind you, and the sisters handled the smallest.
But they were the ones I longed for, their lop-sided heads.

After lunch we went outdoors, see-saws and slides,
sand boxes on both ends of the yard. One boy would
not speak. He sat and stared and I loved him.

But that was nothing, a summer of volunteer distraction.
For years I answered phones, drafted letters, made
important deliveries. I greeted clients and ushered them in.

Eventually I grew tired of these men who thought they mattered.
My hands preferred book jackets and dress patterns, dough,
smooth stones from the stream, sheets fresh from the dryer.

Now, as I grow lovelier, I keep track: the left hand
more Byzantine in its wrinkling, the right one
always sloshing dishwater or deep in soil.

Once, I remember, I sat myself down, finished—
every dish and pan clean, dresses, pillowslips and trousers
pressed and folded, not a plant to pot or a book to shelve.

Now what, I asked myself. Better to keep moving,
always leave a little mess, a few chores to fill the hours
as everything blossoms, withers, dies, season after season.

Wednesday afternoons, now, the skinny girl in her one braid
brings "House and Garden," cookies, a cake nearly baked right.
When I care to, I remember her name.

Evie Safran, of Crozet, writes:

I first read Giavanna Munafo's poem when I was forty-four years old. Last year, I rediscovered it at the age of sixty-seven. It was even more beautiful this second time, because its images had become a mirror of my life and a foreshadowing. I nearly wept.

This past winter was the first season, after twenty-five years of teaching and catering, that I was not working. On a day like too many similar days, I experienced that moment in the poem when the narrator says, "Now what...." I had sorted my recipes, recycled dozens of magazines, made piles of giveaway clothes, and cooked over days and weeks enough food for ten people: "Better to keep moving...."

Better to keep working, I thought. Better to be useful in our youth-obsessed society. For this is the irony of aging: when we are young, we long to fit in; when we grow old, we long to stand out! Sadly, ageism and its biases often thwart our desire to be visible and appreciated for the experiences we've acquired, so that we might yet enhance the lives of the young people we meet.

"I'm getting lovelier by the hour, and the intricacies/ of my skin increase as I speak." Though white-haired and starting to wrinkle, I am "getting lovelier by the hour." It is a loveliness born from a life of singular experiences and relationships, from a sense of trust in my resilience, from a career of making a difference in the lives of children, and from a dedication to learning and to the people I love.

In time, someone may bring me a cake when I can't bake one myself, and I may or may not "remember her name." And like the feelings expressed in this poem, the cake will be bittersweet.

Love's Coming

John Shaw Neilson

Quietly as rosebuds
Talk to the thin air,
Love came so lightly
I knew not he was there.

Quietly as lovers
Creep at the middle moon,
Softly as players tremble
In the tears of a tune;

Quietly as lilies
Their faint vows declare,
Came the shy pilgrim:
I knew not he was there.

Quietly as tears fall
On a wild sin,
Softly as griefs call
In a violin;

Without hail or tempest,
Blue sword or flame,
Love came so lightly
I knew not that he came.

Mary-Grace Rusnak, of Virginia Beach, writes:

Countless hours spent standing at my kitchen sink, washing hands, washing vegetables, washing dishes, gazing out at the changes brought by the seasons in an endless stream of thought. My hands are dutifully constrained by work, yet my mind is free to wander where it wishes, escaping into beauty that soon triumphs over the mundane, making an ordinary life more bearable, if not quietly spectacular.

My nearest poem, "Love's Coming," catches me by surprise each time I read it. It reminds me that I am not alone, not the first to experience the thrill of beauty or creativity coming quietly, taking root, taking wing, even before I know it's there. John Shaw Neilson speaks to me of love, of life, and of art as a way of preserving one's sanity. Neilson provides glimpses of the extraordinary just beneath the surface of the everyday. He reassures me that some facets of life are timeless and easily shared with kindred spirits across miles and centuries.

The Bells

(an excerpt)

Edgar Allan Poe

I.

Hear the sledges with the bells—
Silver bells!
What a world of merriment their melody foretells!
How they tinkle, tinkle, tinkle,
In the icy air of night!
While the stars that oversprinkle
All the heavens, seem to twinkle
With a crystalline delight;
Keeping time, time, time,
In a sort of Runic rhyme.
To the tintinabulation that so musically wells
From the bells, bells, bells, bells,
Bells, bells, bells—
From the jingling and the tinkling of the bells.

IV.

Hear the tolling of the bells—
Iron bells!
What a world of solemn thought their monody compels!
In the silence of the night,
How we shiver with affright
At the melancholy menace of their tone!
For every sound that floats
From the rust within their throats
Is a groan.
And the people—ah, the people—
They that dwell up in the steeple,
All alone,

And who tolling, tolling, tolling,
In that muffled monotone,
Feel a glory in so rolling
On the human heart a stone—
They are neither man nor woman—
They are neither brute nor human—
They are Ghouls:
And their king it is who tolls;
And he rolls, rolls, rolls,
Rolls
A pæan from the bells!
And his merry bosom swells
With the pæan of the bells!
And he dances, and he yells;
Keeping time, time, time,
In a sort of Runic rhyme,
To the pæan of the bells—
Of the bells:
Keeping time, time, time,
In a sort of Runic rhyme,
To the throbbing of the bells—
Of the bells, bells, bells—
To the sobbing of the bells;
Keeping time, time, time,
As he knells, knells, knells,
In a happy Runic rhyme,
To the rolling of the bells—
Of the bells, bells, bells—
To the tolling of the bells,
Of the bells, bells, bells, bells—
Bells, bells, bells—
To the moaning and the groaning of the bells.

⊱⊰⊱

John Urquhart and Elizabeth Urquhart, of Hampton, write:

Poe's poetry contains many powerful images that hang in our minds. This example may suffice: a pane of glass taken from the window of Room 13, West Range, which we learned was on display in the Rotunda of the University of Virginia. According to legend, Poe etched the following stanza into this pane sometime before his unfortunate departure:

> O Thou timid one, do not let thy
> Form slumber within these
> Unhallowed walls,
> For herein lies
> The ghost of an awful crime.

Nevertheless, the poem that will stay with us forever is "The Bells." Many poems can be read silently, alone, but "The Bells" demands to be performed, almost as a piece of music. Indeed, Sergei Rachmaninoff (1873–1943) composed a choral symphony, Op. 35 "The Bells," based on a Russian adaptation of the poem by Konstantin Balmont.

Given a powerful reader, the listener is seized by the rhythm and the sound of the bells. At first, the bells are cheerful and friendly, but as one progresses towards the final stanza, the tone changes, and the final stanza deals with death and the announcement of death by the bells, and it raises the hair on the back of your neck. True Poe.

Since You Asked

for a friend who asked to be in a poem

Lawrence Raab

Since you asked, let's make it dinner
at your house-a celebration
for no reason, which is always
the best occasion. Are you worried
there won't be enough space, enough food?

But in a poem we can do anything we want.
Look how easy it is to add on rooms, to multiply
the wine and chickens. And while we're at it
let's take those trees that died last winter
and bring them back to life.

Things should look pulled together,
and we could use the shade-so even now
they shudder and unfold their bright new leaves.
And now the guests are arriving-everyone
you expected, then others as well:

friends who never became your friends,
the women you didn't marry, all their children.
And the dead-I didn't tell you
but they're always included in these gatherings-
hesitant and shy, they hang back at first

among the blossoming trees.
You have only to say their names,
ask them inside. Everyone will find a place
at your table. What more can I do?
The glasses are filled, the children are quiet.

My friend, it must be time for you to speak.

❧ ❧ ❧

Linda Holtslander, of Loudoun County, writes:

I have read this poem aloud many times; I have read it at literary events and on numerous other occasions. I also keep it in my wallet. Why? Because it would be wonderful if you could really make what the poem says happen.

written on the way to a memorial service for an ex-lover

Rashani Réa

i'm a simple gopi fallen to her knees,
singing endless praises
like the wind
sings through the trees.

filled now with wonderment
distilling into grace,
i find traces of you everywhere
through your ever-present face.

only the flower dies.
its fragrance still remains
and the moon is always full,
even as it wanes.

i know love does to pain
what sunlight does to rain,
in the absence of doership
we're reminded once again

that inherent in each cloud
is a rainbow not-yet-born,
the awakened state is present
even as we mourn.

so let the tears keep flowing
and trust whatever comes,
each moment is a banquet
of abundance, not of crumbs.

৵৵৵

Andrea T., of Blacksburg, writes:

This poem found me at a challenging time in my life and provided me with a sense of gratitude and perspective that gave me peace. At the time I was going through a very painful estrangement from my only sibling; it appeared I had lost that crucial relationship, and I didn't know why. This poem reminded me that, even in times that feel complex, I am a simple gopi. We all are.

I was distracted from my "singing endless praises" by my pain, but it is through this endless singing on our knees, and through acknowledging the wonderment living in our hearts, that we may experience love illuminating and evaporating our pain. Réa shows us that suffering does not banish us to a state of separation, but rather that awareness is present, waiting calmly nearby, throughout our grief. Pain is a doorway, not an obstacle.

The last stanza is the most dear to me. When faced with challenges, we are tempted to believe that the bounty and comfort we don't perceive in the present will be found in the future. Réa shows us that this division between a sparse present and a nourishing future is a false one, and that we can simultaneously grieve and revel. The way this poem vividly illustrates the simultaneity of pain and wonder makes it my nearest poem. Every hour or day that I can remain mindful of the "banquet/ of abundance, not of crumbs" is an hour or day better lived.

Letter to My Principal

Edwin Romond

I came to school late today
and I am sorry.
I do remember your note
about my punctuality
but a calf was born last night
and I found him blinking
into his first morning
and, Sir,
he was so tiny and white,
like a dab of marshmallow
upon the spearmint grass.
So, please understand
I was caught in a sunrise
so gold it turned our barn
to pink and sponged the dew
where the calf lay startled
at the light after life
in the black pond of the womb.
I was set to leave, I swear I was,
but his mother, her eyes dark plums,
began to bathe him with her tongue
moving like a paint brush
up and down his milky face.
And when he gazed at me
and mooed like a nervous bassoon,
what could I do but stay
until he stood on his own
and began to tiptoe
as if the grass were eggs?

ھ۔ھ۔ھ

Bob Young, of Virginia Beach, writes:

I was startled by this "Letter," which I discovered in THE SUN, in December 1988. I'm a poet and a letter-writer; I'm also a big-city kid—New York and Philadelphia. Growing up, I didn't know anything about farms and cattle and birthings, and as far as I recall, I had little interest in such things. I could not have experienced what this student, this principal, this calf and mother had been through. Because of this—or in spite of it—the poem grabbed hold of me. The whole scene was incredibly clear, and so tenderly offered, as in the lines: "And when he gazed at me/ and mooed like a nervous bassoon/ what could I do but stay."

I was a retired medical school teacher in 1991, volunteering at a Quaker school in Virginia Beach with a class of middle-school students. I read the poem with my students and saw how the verses touched them. What a magnificent conversation we had! We wondered what it would be like to witness the birth of a calf. We wondered about the age and the gender of the student, and how he/she might have learned to talk so beautifully. One of the questions I asked them was, "If you were the principal, what would you say to this student about the lateness?" We all agreed that for the moment at least, we would be respectfully speechless.

At a time when the written word seems threatened, letters remain important. This one moves me still. While preparing this essay, I Googled the author and learned that the poem had been set to music by a choral group and could be listened to. Words are lyrical, and good words set to music are a double-decker treat. I know; I had the poem before me and listened to it being sung.

Chicago

Carl Sandburg

Hog Butcher for the World,
  Tool Maker, Stacker of Wheat,
  Player with Railroads and the Nation's Freight Handler;
  Stormy, husky, brawling,
  City of the Big Shoulders:

They tell me you are wicked and I believe them, for I
  have seen your painted women under the gas lamps
  luring the farm boys.
And they tell me you are crooked and I answer: Yes, it
  is true I have seen the gunman kill and go free to
  kill again.
And they tell me you are brutal and my reply is: On the
  faces of women and children I have seen the marks
  of wanton hunger.
And having answered so I turn once more to those who
  sneer at this my city, and I give them back the sneer
  and say to them:
Come and show me another city with lifted head singing
  so proud to be alive and coarse and strong and cunning.
Flinging magnetic curses amid the toil of piling job on
  job, here is a tall bold slugger set vivid against the
  little soft cities;
Fierce as a dog with tongue lapping for action, cunning
  as a savage pitted against the wilderness,
      Bareheaded,
      Shoveling,
      Wrecking,
      Planning,
      Building, breaking, rebuilding,

Under the smoke, dust all over his mouth, laughing with
   white teeth,
Under the terrible burden of destiny laughing as a young
   man laughs,
Laughing even as an ignorant fighter laughs who has
   never lost a battle,
Bragging and laughing that under his wrist is the pulse.
   and under his ribs the heart of the people,
     Laughing!
Laughing the stormy, husky, brawling laughter of
   Youth, half-naked, sweating, proud to be Hog
   Butcher, Tool Maker, Stacker of Wheat, Player with
   Railroads and Freight Handler to the Nation.

Mary E. Burns, of Albemarle County, writes:

My nearest poem is Carl Sandburg's "Chicago." Most likely I first read it in a high school English class. I grew up in a small town, Charlottesville, and yearned for the big city, its "Building, breaking, rebuilding…. Bragging and laughing…." I was ignorant of wickedness, crookedness, and brutality. But I could pretend I was from Chicago or dream of moving there, and believe that I'd be able to handle a big city because I was young, strong, and determined.

This poem's vibrant urban images and language also sang to me. I recall that I loved to read it aloud. Its sounds energized me; I loved its gritty character, its distinctness from classic poems, which I found stilted. This was poetry I could actually like; here was a poet I could appreciate. I sympathized with the terrible beauty of the city and the humanity of its people. As the years passed, the poem continued to exert its influence on me. It never failed to resurrect my memories of "Chicago" and my emotional self as a young woman.

In recent years, after having lived in and visited big cities, but curiously never Chicago, I've returned to reading more poetry in a quieter setting, and I had to find and read "Chicago" again. I had a notion that it would lead me once more into the pleasures of poetry. And it has. I can laugh outright and delight in the "half-naked, sweating, proud to be Hog Butcher, Tool Maker, Stacker of Wheat…." I'm re-energized and look forward to discovering new joys in poetry.

Richard II, Act II, Scene 1
John of Gaunt's Monologue
(an excerpt)

William Shakespeare

Methinks I am a prophet new inspired
And thus expiring do foretell of him:
His rash fierce blaze of riot cannot last,
For violent fires soon burn out themselves;
Small showers last long, but sudden storms are short;
He tires betimes that spurs too fast betimes;
With eager feeding food doth choke the feeder:
Light vanity, insatiate cormorant,
Consuming means, soon preys upon itself.
This royal throne of kings, this scepter'd isle,
This earth of majesty, this seat of Mars,
This other Eden, demi-paradise,
This fortress built by Nature for herself
Against infection and the hand of war,
This happy breed of men, this little world,
This precious stone set in the silver sea,
Which serves it in the office of a wall,
Or as a moat defensive to a house,
Against the envy of less happier lands,
This blessed plot, this earth, this realm, this England...

❧❧❧

Jessica Malicki Blaisus, of Portsmouth, writes:

As a girl, I came across a poem by Jane Yolen about unicorn horns that changed my life forever. I showed the poem to my mother, who realized it was an homage to Shakespeare's Richard II and introduced me to the Bard. My mother opened my world to what I know now as meter and rhetoric. I memorized John of Gaunt's monologue for fun — and discovered I wanted more.

When I was fourteen, I auditioned at a local community theatre. I told the director that I had no experience, then stumbled halfway through Hamlet's "To be or not to be" before I had to stop and start again from the beginning. Despite, or perhaps because of, my persistence and honesty, the director cast me. I was hooked. I auditioned for every Shakespeare production I could squeeze into my busy schedule. Opportunity gave me knowledge, and knowledge gave me opportunities.

What moves me is how Shakespeare lets us see England through John of Gaunt's eyes and fall in love with a country many of us have never seen. In addition, I've learned to identify the linguistic nuances of why the piece speaks to me, such as the link between "inspired" and "expiring" through their common Latin root of "spirare;" the antithesis of the masculine "seat of Mars" and the feminine fortress "built by Nature for herself/ Against infection and the hand of war;" the climax that builds to "this England," which is the height of Gaunt's praise and embodies, in one word, all the words that have come before.

If asked why I liked the poem when I first encountered it, I would have said that it was "beautiful." Knowing the mechanics of that beauty has only increased my appreciation. Still, when I close my eyes and let the words roll off my tongue, I do not see the verses and all of their complexity. I see England.

Rinsed with Gold, Endless, Walking the Fields

Robert Siegel

Let this day's air praise the Lord—
Rinsed with gold, endless, walking the fields,
Blue and bearing the clouds like censers,
Holding the sun like a single note
Running through all things, a *basso profundo*
Rousing the birds to an endless chorus.

Let the river throw itself down before him,
The rapids laugh and flash with his praise,
Let the lake tremble about its edges
And gather itself in one clear thought
To mirror the heavens and the reckless gulls
That swoop and rise on its glittering shores.

Let the lawn burn continually before him
A green flame, and the tree's shadow
Sweep over it like the baton of a conductor,
Let winds hug the housecorners and woodsmoke
Sweeten the world with her invisible dress,
Let the cricket wind his heartspring
And draw the night by like a child's toy.

Let the tree stand and thoughtfully consider
His presence as its leaves dip and row
The long sea of winds, as sun and moon
Unfurl and decline like contending flags.

Let blackbirds quick as knives praise the Lord,
Let the sparrow line the moon for her nest
And pick the early sun for her cherry,
Let her slide on the outgoing breath of evening,
Telling of raven and dove,
The quick flutters, homings to the green houses.

Let the worm climb a winding stair,
Let the mole offer no sad explanation
As he paddles aside the dark from his nose,
Let the dog tug on the leash of his bark
The startled cat electrically hiss,
And the snake sign her name in the dust

In joy. For it is he who underlies
The rock from its liquid foundation,
The sharp contraries of the giddy atom,
The unimaginable curve of space,
Time pulling like a patient string,
And gravity, fiercest of natural loves.

At his laughter, splendor riddles the night,
Galaxies swarm from a secret hive,
Mountains split and crawl for aeons
To huddle again, and planets melt
In the last tantrum of a dying star.

At his least signal spring shifts
Its green patina over half the earth,
Deserts whisper themselves over the cities,
Polar caps widen and wither like flowers.

In his stillness rock shifts, root probes,
The spider tenses her geometrical ego,
The larva dreams in the heart of the peachwood,
The child's pencil makes a shaky line,
The dog sighs and settles deeper,
And a smile takes hold like the feet of a bird.

Sit straight, let the air ride down your backbone,
Let your lungs unfold like a field of roses,
Your eyes hang the sun and moon between them,

Your hands weigh the sky in even balance,
Your tongue, swiftest of members, release a word
Spoken at conception to the sanctum of genes,
And each breath rise sinuous with praise.

Let your feet move to the rhythm of your pulse
(Your joints like pearls and rubies he has hidden),
And your hands float high on the tide of your feelings.
Now, shout from the stomach, hoarse with music,
Give gladness and joy back to the Lord,
Who, sly as a milkweed, takes root in your heart.

Suzanne Underwood Rhodes, of Virginia Beach, writes:

The poem I have selected as being nearest is one that has sung to me from the moment I first heard it read aloud by the author, the late Robert Siegel, back in the 1980s at King College in Bristol, Tennessee, where he was the distinguished guest for the Staley lecture series. The poem is "Rinsed with Gold, Endless, Walking the Fields." The title announces that we are in for a dance with beauty. A summons to praise, Siegel's twelve stanzas move us with sensory delight as we admire each discrete and personified element of creation.

This is a world ablaze with the glory of God, where the poet imagines the playful mind of the Maker as immersed in every mote of his making—an act as small as a child's pencil making its "shaky line" or as grand as galaxies that "swarm from a secret hive." For all the music and gathered images that make me smile on every reading, for the poem's formal pattern that imparts dignity appropriate for its holy purpose, for its delightful sound associations, and perhaps most of all, for its grasp of God, not as a remote force but as a personal presence inhabiting his creation—for these reasons, "Rinsed with Gold..." sings on.

Life Is Motion

Wallace Stevens

In Oklahoma,
Bonnie and Josie,
Dressed in calico,
Danced around a stump.
They cried,
"Ohoyaho,
Ohoo"...
Celebrating the marriage
Of flesh and air.

Derek Kannemeyer, of Richmond, writes:

I grew up in England. American poetry was an exotic mystery, its study forbidden. I do not exaggerate. I recall my high school English teacher, whom I revered, finding us in his classroom at lunch one day, discussing the Paul Simon song "Dangling Conversation," whose text we'd written on the board. He nodded with amusement until he reached the lines "And you read your Emily Dickinson, and I my Robert Frost," at which point he exploded. The term "cultural imperialism" wasn't yet in vogue, but that was his charge: we English were besieged, and Dickinson, Frost were sniper fire.

But this was the sixties, and we were rebel children. I had my favorite English poems by heart— Wordsworth, Blake, Tennyson, Hopkins—and those enemy Americans felt utterly alien. But how I liked to sneak peeks! And the next year, in my college library, discovering Wallace Stevens, I fell headlong in love. I can't say I understood him; I didn't expect to understand Americans. But that music! That vigor of image! That barbarously rapturous tone! Well, many poems in HARMONIUM seduced me, not all of them so ecstatic, but this was my favorite.

Learning to read Stevens—his hunger for the imagination to reanimate the real—has enlarged my appreciation of it, but it's at the first, literal, vividly specific level that the poem sings most fiercely to me. Its rhythmical chant around a central stump. Its pleasure in breath, in motion, in the body's raw, savage cry.

The Snow Man

Wallace Stevens

One must have a mind of winter
To regard the frost and the boughs
Of the pine-trees crusted with snow;

And have been cold a long time
To behold the junipers shagged with ice,
The spruces rough in the distant glitter

Of the January sun; and not to think
Of any misery in the sound of the wind,
In the sound of a few leaves,

Which is the sound of the land
Full of the same wind
That is blowing in the same bare place

For the listener, who listens in the snow,
And, nothing himself, beholds
Nothing that is not there and the nothing that is.

Warren Meredith Harris, of Abingdon, writes:

There are two reasons why Wallace Stevens's "The Snow Man" resonates with me. First, it describes "a mind of winter," a term that in a sense fits my own. The mind in the poem, after contemplation, becomes able to accept the "bare" world for what it is. It arrives at a quiet place beyond the awareness of biting cold and "misery" that the winter wind represents. But the poem also becomes a celebration in words — as all great poems do — in this case, of austere beauty, of tree branches filigreed against the winter sky, my favorite natural scene.

The other reason has to do with its powerful portrayal of reality. It tells me this physical world is not free-standing. The poem is a verbal analogy of those pictures carefully designed to allow viewers to switch their perception of what is figure and what is background. In one well-known visual example, viewers usually first notice a white vase on a black background. But as they continue to look, they see two symmetrical faces in black profile looking at each other on a white background. Both perceptions are equally "real."

In "The Snow Man," what corresponds to the white, obvious vase in the picture is winter's "this world" reality. The "nothing" of the poem, referring both to the self and the world around us, corresponds to the black of the picture, what we normally do not focus on. But when Stevens describes it as "the nothing that is," he shows it to be just as real, just as worthy of the verb "is," as ordinary reality. Philosophers have pointed out that this "nothing" is literally "no thing," that is, not a being, but rather, the ground of being. For me, "The Snow Man" brings to mind reality's (back)ground and makes it the foreground.

There Will Come Soft Rains

Sara Teasdale

There will come soft rains and the smell of the ground,
And swallows circling with their shimmering sound;

And frogs in the pools singing at night,
And wild plum trees in tremulous white;

Robins will wear their feathery fire
Whistling their whims on a low fence-wire;

And not one will know of the war, not one
Will care at last when it is done.

Not one would mind, neither bird nor tree,
If mankind perished utterly;

And Spring herself, when she woke at dawn,
Would scarcely know that we were gone.

Isaiah Johnson, of Petersburg, writes:

I first noticed "There Will Come Soft Rains" by Sara Teasdale in a video game, and I immediately became interested in this poem. Whenever I get sad or disconcerted, I look to this poem and it calms me. I often focus on the last verses of the poem: "And Spring herself, when she woke at dawn,/ Would scarcely know that we were gone." I like those lines because of the personification of spring, and because they provoke thoughts of changing seasons after humanity has died. I'm also drawn to the mention of war, and the idea of the end of mankind, as a Book of Eli type disaster.

In the video game Fallout 3, where the poem appears, it is two hundred years after a nuclear war. There is a robot whose job, at one time, was to recite this poem to children as a bedtime story. Two hundred years later, he's still at work and will recite the poem for anyone who wants to hear it. It fits the feel of the game almost perfectly, and the poem may have even inspired the game.

I find this poem calming and very apt for certain situations. Also, as a sophomore at the Appomattox Regional Governor's School with a focus area on Literary Arts, I want to write and will continue writing throughout my life, using poems like this, as well as fiction, to inspire me to write my own poems and stories.

Now Sleeps the Crimson Petal, Now the White

Alfred, Lord Tennyson

Now sleeps the crimson petal, now the white;
Nor waves the cypress in the palace walk;
Nor winks the gold fin in the porphyry font:
The firefly wakens: waken thou with me.

Now droops the milk-white peacock like a ghost,
And like a ghost she glimmers on to me.

Now lies the Earth all Danaë to the stars,
And all thy heart lies open unto me.

Now slides the silent meteor on, and leaves
A shining furrow, as thy thoughts in me.

Now folds the lily all her sweetness up,
And slips into the bosom of the lake.
So fold thyself, my dearest, thou, and slip
Into my bosom and be lost in me.

Christine Sparks, of James City County, writes:

When I was a child my mother would play the piano. Her favorite song was "Now Sleeps the Crimson Petal, Now the White." This song's lyrics were written by Alfred, Lord Tennyson during the Victorian era. Even as a child, I loved his passion, variegated with color: "the crimson…the white…the gold fin," and "the milk-white peacock like a ghost…." In the silence of the night, Tennyson's words would whisper to me: "And slips/ into the bosom of the lake." How lyrical they sounded!

As we created our musical duet, my mother and I were like the secrets of the night, perfectly content. Even now, when I read or sing the poem, I feel a ghostlike union with my mother, who has since passed. The poem did more for us than inspire; it united.

The taste of chocolate, like faith

Hilary Tham

How can you describe the taste
of chocolate to one who has never
tasted chocolate? The truth of chocolate
can be known only by sucking it; the taste
is not to be found in words, but in the mouth
in the melting of butter, sugar, cocoa, milk
on the tongue and in the memory of
one who has eaten chocolate.

How can I describe my faith to another?
I could say it is this sense of nothingness
that nourishes the soul. This sense of
an inner world, concealed, a world that is not
our world, not perceived, not communicable.
I could say faith is a soap bubble
holding light.

We say Zen, or Enlightenment, or
Ayin, the word Jewish mystics use
for the human joining with the light of God.
Not God, only the shadow light that
emanates from holiness, the hollowness where
God was and now is not.

When we try to communicate the essence
of God, we reach the limits of language.
Words are inadequate as cupped hands to scoop sea
water, saying Ocean is salty, vast, deep,
Ocean is blue, green, turquoise,
aquamarine, all colors of light and dark.
The water in our hands leaks away, colorless.

Jacqueline Jules, of Arlington, writes:

Not everyone finds sustenance from faith. My husband shares my religion in a cultural sense, but not my belief in a Supreme Being. After painful discussions, we have agreed not to open up this topic in our home anymore.

In "The taste of chocolate, like faith," Hilary Tham eloquently expresses why I cannot explain an essential part of my being to the person dearest to me, the man who is not only my husband, but also my best friend. We share anxieties, insecurities, and social inadequacies. We discuss intimate details of each other's health. But we cannot talk rationally about why I need to pray—why my belief in God gives me the courage to live.

In her poem, Tham compares this dilemma to the taste of chocolate. You cannot describe it to someone who has never tasted it. You can say it is good, but "the taste/ is not to be found in words, but in the mouth." When speaking of God, we do reach "the limits of language" and "Words are inadequate as cupped hands to scoop sea." Tham suggests that "faith is a soap bubble/ holding light." This astounding image nourishes my core.

The power of poetry lies in its ability to encapsulate profound emotion within a few well-chosen words. In "The taste of chocolate, like faith," Tham gives my trust in God a voice as iridescent as the rainbow light contained in a floating sphere too delicate to touch.

Chanson d'automne

Paul Verlaine

The long sobs
Of the violins
Of Autumn
Wound my heart
With a monotonous
Languor.

All choked
And pale, when
The hour chimes,
I remember
Days of old
And I cry

And I'm going
On an ill wind
That carries me
Here and there,
As if a
Dead leaf.

John A. Bray, of Williamsburg, writes:

The first verse of "Chanson d'automne" was broadcast in two parts by the BBC to the French Resistance in the opening days of June 1944 to alert them to the imminent Allied invasion at Normandy. This scene was re-created in the motion picture, THE LONGEST DAY, a film about the first twenty-four hours of the invasion. The words have remained in my memory, even in French, since viewing the movie many years ago, in 1963.

There are other reasons why this poem has remained in my memory. "Chanson d'automne," one of the best-known poems in the French language, captures, exactly, the seasonal melancholy that often afflicts us when the chill, drab days of fall steal upon us. The author's use of rhyme (in the original version) and other stylistic devices, such as assonance and pause, enhances the meaning of each word and captures Verlaine's sad view of growing old.

Few poems have influenced me as much as this one for its employment of clear imagery and its ability to convey the author's intent, through just the right selection and combination of words. As an author of fiction and as one who has dabbled in poetry infrequently, I am moved by "Autumn Song." I appreciate the way the words and their precise placement evoke an atmosphere of beauty and mournfulness of soul. That the poem was used on such a critical—and somber—moment in history only strengthens its hold.

Who Has Known Heights

Mary Brent Whiteside

Who has known heights and depths shall not again
Know peace—not as the calm heart knows
Low, ivied walls; a garden close;
And though he tread the humble ways of men
He shall not speak the common tongue again.
Who has known heights shall bear forever more
An incommunicable thing
That hurts his heart, as if a wing
Beat at the portal, challenging;
And yes—lured by the gleam his vision wore—
Who once has trodden stars seeks peace no more.

Wheston Chancellor Grove, of Williamsburg, writes:

I don't want to know the impetus behind Mary Brent Whiteside's "Who Has Known Heights." The poem is given with certainty from a place outside the narrator's loss. A return to all that was and came before, "the gleam [of] vision" worn, elicits profound longing and the knowledge that this feeling is permanent company. As a poet and writer myself, I find that it conveys a sense of immeasurable loss. Of being blinded from seeing, or touching upon too much. To know and experience such heights and return from the rafters renders all else anticlimactic.

Some things affect us so deeply that to attempt to give them form through direct words would fail to capture the essence. Whiteside speaks indirectly; we are given modifiers, but never is the source of her poem explicitly revealed. Quietly it reminds us of the heightened passions relevant to an amorous state of being.

I once endured a love affair that erased all others: the apex of affection and desire, an equilibrium of sight — to love and be loved. A very rare communion. Her name was Magdalena, "Leni." She lived and so did I. We came from different times and different places. But we were here in "this time." One day this is what will remain.

A restlessness, a constant reminder of amputated peace, resounds with the line "as if a wing/ Beat at the portal, challenging." I envision a hummingbird, a fluttering urgency, refusing to mend the intimate chamber of one's deepest emotions. There are places none may penetrate and which one will not disclose. Like a "garden close," shrouded in ivy walls, certain "attachments can never be grasped," as Proust would have his Charles Swann speak.

However, there does exist a universal condition, this shared capacity for emotion to which Mary Brent Whiteside speaks. Though her intention may be different from what her words evoke in us, it nonetheless draws parallels in our lives.

The Red Wheelbarrow

William Carlos Williams

so much depends
upon

a red wheel
barrow

glazed with rain
water

beside the white
chickens.

ॐॐॐ

Christy Lumm, of Newport News, writes:

Enigmatic and elusive, "The Red Wheelbarrow" had always provided me and my high school classes stimulus for fun discussions. I was a new teacher, eager to introduce students to thought-provoking poems. The meaning of the poem lay in its simple images—or so we had decided.

Now I know better. I had been driving home in rural northern Michigan thirty-five years ago, on a damp fall day after a rain, towards the end of the peak leaf season. My direction was due west, into the late afternoon sun. Worries weighed on me; my two-year-old son slept, strapped into his child seat behind me. We drove through the hilly farmland and reached a ridge overlooking miles of rolling hills. Without warning raw beauty spread before me in all directions. I pulled the car over to the side of the road and turned the engine off.

Glowing silver outlined the rain clouds over the west; the cleansed air brought them within reach. On a slight rise, a white clapboard farmhouse sat on pulsing green grass, a front-yard maple tree aflame in leaves. Beyond the farmhouse lay its red barn. The rain had washed away any impurities, so what I saw was perfection glowing in the setting sun. My worries vanished. William Carlos Williams's poem formed in my mind, as if he were saying: "This is exactly what I was writing about: the transformative power of beauty. Take it in! It won't last!"

Now, when I teach this poem, I explain how Williams was a New Jersey doctor. Weighed down with worries for a beloved patient, he had gone to a window to think. What he saw outside—a red wheelbarrow, the white chickens—restored his spirit. He was able to help his patient without despairing. So much depends upon our pausing to breathe in the simple, restorative wonders around us.

Lines written a few miles above Tintern Abbey
(an excerpt)

William Wordsworth

Though absent long,
These beauteous forms have not been to me
As is a landscape to a blind man's eye:
But oft, in lonely rooms, and 'mid the din
Of towns and cities, I have owed to them
In hours of weariness, sensations sweet,
Felt in the blood, and felt along the heart;
And passing even into my purer mind,
With tranquil restoration: — feelings too
Of unremembered pleasure: such, perhaps,
As have no slight or trivial influence
On that best portion of a good man's life,
His little, nameless, unremembered, acts
Of kindness and of love. Nor less, I trust,
To them I may have owed another gift,
Of aspect more sublime; that blessed mood,
In which the burthen of the mystery,
In which the heavy and the weary weight
Of all this unintelligible world,
Is lighten'd: — that serene and blessed mood,
In which the affections gently lead us on, —
Until, the breath of this corporeal frame
And even the motion of our human blood
Almost suspended, we are laid asleep
In body, and become a living soul:
While with an eye made quiet by the power
Of harmony, and the deep power of joy,
We see into the life of things.

If this
Be but a vain belief—yet oh, how oft

In darkness and amid the many shapes
Of joyless daylight; when the fretful stir
Unprofitable, and the fever of the world,
Have hung upon the beatings of my heart—
How oft, in spirit, have I turned to thee,
O sylvan Wye! thou wanderer thro' the woods,
How often has my spirit turned to thee!
And now, with gleams of half-extinguished thought,
With many recognitions dim and faint,
And somewhat of a sad perplexity,
The picture of the mind revives again:
While here I stand, not only with the sense
Of present pleasure, but with pleasing thoughts
That in this moment there is life and food
For future years.

⤙⤙⤙

Christopher Scalia, of Norton, writes:

"Tintern Abbey" has been near to me since I first read it as a student at William & Mary. In it, Wordsworth describes returning to the Welsh countryside he hasn't visited in years and relates not only the natural beauty of the place, but also the intellectual and spiritual influence it had on him when he was away. His memories were a source of strength and beauty, and he's confident that his "present pleasure" will also provide "life and food/ For future years."

Wordsworth's poem has always reminded me of how I felt when, growing up, I'd explore the woods and parks around Northern Virginia. It captures the excitement and wonder I experienced when my friends and I used to hop along the creek by our houses and follow it to the Potomac, where we'd take in the views of the river as it surged or meandered. And just as Wordsworth found "tranquil restoration" long after his visits, I still gain comfort and strength from memories of wandering along (and off) trails, climbing hills for the best views of the waterfalls, taking it all in alone or with an old friend.

Strange, but even though I didn't read "Tintern Abbey" until college, it has become part of my childhood. I think of those woods whenever I read the poem, and I think of the poem whenever I return to those woods. Wordsworth evokes the power of place and childhood, even very far away and much later on — which happens to be a lot like the power of a great poem.

Emotion

Brother, I would have carried you
on my shoulders 'til the horizon bent for us
and our forest dawned along its edge.
Imagine, and the maples stoop to greet you,
saying welcome back,
welcome home.

Victoria White, the poet

There's something about this poem...that really reaches me.
Each time I read it, I feel a huge sense of urgency
to go help someone, to go help my sister,
to go help the brother I don't even have.

Nathan Salle, the reader

For My Children, Each of You

Joseph F. Awad

When I could bundle you off to bed,
When you wore pajamas with toes,
I'd look into your room at night—
Moments only your angel knows.

You made me rich. I hoarded you
As a miser in the dark of night
Counts and recounts his stacks of gold,
Gazing upon them with delight.

I would wonder at the windowed grace
Of starlight haloing starlight hair
Or china curve of brow or cheek.
Hovering I would make a prayer.

You are grown and gone. The house is still.
I look in your room at an empty bed.
I bless you and blindly make a prayer
That stargrace haloes your heavy head.

ॐॐॐ

Edward W. Lull, of Williamsburg, writes:

Poetry played no real role in my growing up or my education. I became acquainted with it only to the extent that it was required of me in English classes. As a result, I carried no lifelong love or relationship with any poem or particular poet. That came much later.

As a young adult and junior naval officer, I knew I wanted to be a father, but I realized that to be a good parent and a career naval officer would require special commitment and teamwork with my young wife, who shared my parenthood desires. The birth of our first child, a son, was greeted with great joy, enthusiasm, and hope; he lived just one day. We fought off depression by strengthening our commitment to have a family, recognizing the blessings that children are to loving parents. We carried this love and commitment through the birth and growing up of our three children. After they left, even their bedrooms held oceans of nostalgia for me. Then grandchildren began to appear.

When I began writing poetry and joined the Poetry Society of Virginia in 1998, Joseph Awad had completed three years as President of the Society, and soon afterward would be appointed Poet Laureate of Virginia. I felt obliged to purchase his recently published book LEANING TO HEAR THE MUSIC. Alone, when I read the dedication poem, I was brought to tears. Despite our different childhoods, educations, and careers, Awad expresses a love of family, deep religious faith, and nostalgia, as he visualizes one of his beautiful children in a now-empty bedroom, that move me as no other poet has.

How old is my heart, how old?

Christopher John Brennan

How old is my heart, how old is my heart,
and did I ever go forth with song when the morn was new?
I seem to have trod on many ways: I seem to have left
I know not how many homes; and to leave each
was still to leave a portion of mine own heart,
of my old heart whose life I had spent to make that home
and all I had was regret, and a memory.

So I sit and muse in this wayside harbour and wait
till I hear the gathering cry of the ancient winds and again
I must up and out and leave the embers of the hearth
to crumble silently into white ash and dust,
and see the road stretch bare and pale before me: again
my garment and my home shall be the enveloping winds
and my heart be fill'd wholly with their old pitiless cry.

Serena Fusek, of Newport News, writes:

Christopher Brennan was born in Sydney. I found his poem "How old is my heart…" while browsing through an anthology of Australian poets. I was thirteen or fourteen—and very impressionable.

The poem is part of a series called "The Wanderer," spoken in the voice of one who is deliberately homeless, who cannot settle, perhaps because he sees that walls are no protection against "the enveloping winds."

I copied out the whole series, but "How old is my heart…" is the poem that caught my imagination. It has accompanied me down the years, and both the poem and I have grown richer for it.

I like the way the poem uses a repetition of Os to set the mood in the first line. They sound like a moan that echoes both the speaker's sorrow and the sound of the unrelenting wind. It is a line I often hear in the back of my mind.

Although the voice is of someone who truly tramped the roads, wearing out shoe leather and his soul, the poem can be understood metaphorically. When the winds come up, each of us is driven out of our niche into the next phase or the next place in our life. Do we still go forth with song?

The Great Lover

Rupert Brooke

I have been so great a lover: filled my days
So proudly with the splendour of Love's praise,
The pain, the calm, and the astonishment,
Desire illimitable, and still content,
And all dear names men use, to cheat despair,
For the perplexed and viewless streams that bear
Our hearts at random down the dark of life.
Now, ere the unthinking silence on that strife
Steals down, I would cheat drowsy Death so far,
My night shall be remembered for a star
That outshone all the suns of all men's days.
Shall I not crown them with immortal praise
Whom I have loved, who have given me, dared with me
High secrets, and in darkness knelt to see—
The inenarrable godhead of delight?
Love is a flame: —we have beaconed the world's night.
A city: —and we have built it, these and I.
An emperor: —we have taught the world to die.
So, for their sakes I loved, ere I go hence,
And the high cause of Love's magnificence,
And to keep loyalties young, I'll write those names
Golden for ever, eagles, crying flames,
And set them as a banner, that men may know,
To dare the generations, burn, and blow
Out on the wind of Time, shining and streaming....

These I have loved:
          White plates and cups, clean-gleaming,
Ringed with blue lines; and feathery, faery dust;
Wet roofs, beneath the lamp-light; the strong crust
Of friendly bread; and many-tasting food;
Rainbows; and the blue bitter smoke of wood;

And radiant raindrops couching in cool flowers;
And flowers themselves, that sway through sunny hours,
Dreaming of moths that drink them under the moon;
Then, the cool kindliness of sheets, that soon
Smooth away trouble; and the rough male kiss
Of blankets; grainy wood; live hair that is
Shining and free; blue-massing clouds; the keen
Unpassioned beauty of a great machine;
The benison of hot water; furs to touch;
The good smell of old clothes; and other such—
The comfortable smell of friendly fingers,
Hair's fragrance, and the musty reek that lingers
About dead leaves and last year's ferns....
                              Dear names,
And thousand other throng to me! Royal flames;
Sweet water's dimpling laugh from tap or spring;
Holes in the ground; and voices that do sing;
Voices in laughter, too; and body's pain,
Soon turned to peace; and the deep-panting train;
Firm sands; the little dulling edge of foam
That browns and dwindles as the wave goes home;
And washen stones, gay for an hour; the cold
Graveness of iron; moist black earthen mould;
Sleep; and high places; footprints in the dew;
And oaks; and brown horse-chestnuts, glossy-new;
And new-peeled sticks; and shining pools on grass;—
All these have been my loves. And these shall pass,
Whatever passes not, in the great hour,
Nor all my passion, all my prayers, have power
To hold them with me through the gate of Death.
They'll play deserter, turn with the traitor breath,
Break the high bond we made, and sell Love's trust
And sacramented covenant to the dust.
—Oh, never a doubt but, somewhere, I shall wake,
And give what's left of love again, and make
New friends, now strangers....

> But the best I've known
> Stays here, and changes, breaks, grows old, is blown
> About the winds of the world, and fades from brains
> Of living men, and dies.
>
> Nothing remains.

> O dear my loves, O faithless, once again
> This one last gift I give: that after men
> Shall know, and later lovers, far-removed,
> Praise you, 'All these were lovely'; say, 'He loved.'

✌ ✌ ✌

Daryl Ann Beeghley, of Lebanon, writes:

At the age of sixteen I fell in love with a man who could never love me back. And I love him still.

He was a poet and a soldier, born in the land of my fathers (he would one day describe himself as "a dust whom England bore, shaped, made aware..."). His words mesmerized me from the start. His intoxication with life permeated my senses.

I fell in love that day, there at my desk, right in the middle of ancient Miss Davis's British Literature class. We read Rupert Brooke's poem "The Great Lover," and I knew from that first moment nothing would ever be the same. I would share his loves, his longings, his way of seeing. I would search for new delights that would delight him too.

Most importantly, I would forever long for words that distill life, for poetry.

When I find myself adrift in life's current, these words pull me back on course, quiet my soul, and remind me to open my eyes, open my heart. To lose myself in the wonder all around me. To be in love with life: with my life. To be such a lover as to cheat drowsy death myself, when and wherever he finds me.

Rupert's words renew the longing in my heart to leave my own legacy of words, that they might one day call another soul to join the dance and say, "She loved."

The Donkey

G. K. Chesterton

When fishes flew and forests walked
  And figs grew upon thorn,
Some moment when the moon was blood
  Then surely I was born.

With monstrous head and sickening cry
  And ears like errant wings,
The devil's walking parody
  On all four-footed things.

The tattered outlaw of the earth,
  Of ancient crooked will;
Starve, scourge, deride me: I am dumb,
  I keep my secret still.

Fools! For I also had my hour;
  One far fierce hour and sweet:
There was a shout about my ears,
  And palms before my feet.

Gillian Dawson, of York County, writes:

This poem was in THE OXFORD BOOK OF ENGLISH VERSE we used in our English Literature class at the boarding school I attended in England. I read it for the first time when I was about ten years old and we were studying poetry. Our homework assignment was to write a short essay explaining what we thought the poem was about and why we did or did not like it.

At first I thought the poem was all about the day some donkey escaped from his cruel master, who pursued him, shouting. But then, I thought, why the palms? Soon I realized the donkey in the poem was the donkey that Jesus rode to Jerusalem on the day we call Palm Sunday, and that the shouts were actually "hosannas." I was so proud of myself for having figured out the poem's meaning that I fell in love with the poem and learned it by heart. And I have never forgotten it.

Not only is the poem a brilliant description of all donkeys who bear our burdens, but in a deeper sense, it implies that all creatures, even the lowliest, deserve kindness and respect, because we never know what great secrets their lives hold. One uplifting experience, one singular moment, can completely change a self-image.

The last verse paints a dramatic scene with a precise economy of words. Chesterton knew that his readers would recognize the story. He did not need to say more in this beautiful, symbolic climax to the poem.

if i should

Lucille Clifton

enter the darkest room
in my house and speak
with my own voice, at last,
about its awful furniture,
pulling apart the covering
over the dusty bodies; the randy
father, the husband holding ice
in his hand like a blessing,
the mother bleeding into herself
and the small imploding girl,
i say if i should walk into
that web, who will come flying
after me, leaping tall buildings?
you?

Sydney Sylvester, of Hopewell, writes:

When I was growing up, I loved to pick favorites. Favorite color, favorite candy, favorite animal. I could never decide my favorite poem, though. I read a wide variety of poets: the classics, the modernists. But I never found a poem that I might consider nearest to me.

One day, my poetry teacher assigned my class a book to read: BLESSING THE BOATS by Lucille Clifton. I had never heard of this poet or the book before, so naturally I was interested. When I began to read I immediately enjoyed her poems. They were bold and sassy, as if the author had no limits when she was writing. She wrote in a style I'd never seen before.

About halfway through the book I came across the poem, "if i should." It seemed so original to me—the way it read, with no periods, like a casual conversation, even the lack of capitalization which made all the words appear equally important. Not only that. The poem is actually addressed to Clark Kent! Who would have thought of writing to Clark Kent! I'd never read anything so audacious and up front. I felt as if Clifton were talking directly to me, rather than writing a poem for someone else.

"if i should" spoke to me in a way no poem ever had before; it opened my eyes to other styles of poetry—many more than I had imagined. Poems didn't have to be traditional. They could be daring and even intimidating. In just thirteen lines, Lucille Clifton had fully commanded my attention and my heart.

Forgetfulness

Billy Collins

The name of the author is the first to go
followed obediently by the title, the plot,
the heartbreaking conclusion, the entire novel
which suddenly becomes one you have never read,
                    never even heard of,

as if, one by one, the memories you used to harbor
decided to retire to the southern hemisphere of the brain,
to a little fishing village where there are no phones.

Long ago you kissed the names of the nine muses goodbye
and watched the quadratic equation pack its bag,
and even now as you memorize the order of the planets,

something else is slipping away, a state flower perhaps,
the address of an uncle, the capital of Paraguay.

Whatever it is you are struggling to remember,
it is not poised on the tip of your tongue
or even lurking in some obscure corner of your spleen.

It has floated away down a dark mythological river
whose name begins with an L as far as you can recall,
well on your own way to oblivion where you will join those
who have even forgotten how to swim and how to ride a bicycle.

No wonder you rise in the middle of the night
to look up the date of a famous battle in a book on war.
No wonder the moon in the window seems to have drifted
out of a love poem that you used to know by heart.

❧❧❧

Martha Dillard, of Sinking Creek, writes:

Few poems stick fully in my memory, including this one called "Forgetfulness." However, I have quoted the first lines to many people in the past ten years and laugh every time I do so. In 2002 I gave Collins's book to my mother for her 91st birthday. She loved poetry and read it often. As she neared her 101st birthday, she left us, and I now have the book to remember her by. Her bookmark was at the page of this poem and will remain there to remind me of the many times we laughed together about forgetting things.

Come Little Leaves

George Cooper

"Come, little leaves," said the wind one day,
"Come over the meadows with me, and play;
Put on your dresses of red and gold;
Summer is gone, and the days grow cold."

Soon as the leaves heard the wind's loud call,
Down they came fluttering, one and all;
Over the brown fields they danced and flew,
Singing the sweet little songs they knew.

"Cricket, good-bye, we've been friends so long;
Little brook, sing us your farewell song,
Say you're sorry to see us go;
Ah! you are sorry, right well we know.

"Dear little lambs, in your fleecy fold,
Mother will keep you from harm and cold;
Fondly we've watched you in vale and glade;
Say, will you dream of our loving shade?"

Dancing and whirling the little leaves went;
Winter had called them and they were content—
Soon fast asleep in their earthy beds,
The snow laid a soft mantle over their heads.

Laura J. Bobrow, of Leesburg, writes:

Some days I would notice it, the deformed tip of mother's ring finger, the result of an encounter between a kitchen knife and a raw duck to be scraped in the early days of marriage. I'd see it as she held a cup, her pinky crooked as a sign that she was a lady of fashion, or when she'd urge, "Waste not, want not," as she brandished a translucent apple peel for approbation.

I'd see it when she recited, unfailingly, "Come Little Leaves" each fall, while the wind whipped them up in swirling spirals from the lawn. Her forefinger was a baton conducting the rhythmic cadence of a schoolgirl's memorized words.

somewhere i have never travelled,gladly beyond

e.e.cummings

somewhere i have never travelled,gladly beyond
any experience,your eyes have their silence:
in your most frail gesture are things which enclose me,
or which i cannot touch because they are too near

your slightest look easily will unclose me
though i have closed myself as fingers,
you open always petal by petal myself as Spring opens
(touching skilfully,mysteriously)her first rose

or if your wish be to close me,i and
my life will shut very beautifully,suddenly,
as when the heart of this flower imagines
the snow carefully everywhere descending;

nothing which we are to perceive in this world equals
the power of your intense fragility:whose texture
compels me with the colour of its countries,
rendering death and forever with each breathing

(i do not know what it is about you that closes
and opens;only something in me understands
the voice of your eyes is deeper than all roses)
nobody,not even the rain, has such small hands

⁓⁓⁓

Gillian Huang-Tiller, of Wise, writes:

Many things feel near and dear in our life, but for the nearest poem, I must take Cummings's sensuous love poem to my heart. It depicts a journey into love moved by the power of the beloved's gaze, and it is crafted with words of simplicity—"open," "close," "fingers," "hands," "heart," "rose"...—which endear my feelings by their mere sounds between my lips.

The repeated imagery of love's "look," opening and closing or enclosing the heart of the lover like a flower unfolds, or like a seasonal cycle—Spring blooming, Winter enfolding—further mesmerizes me. I feel the poem intimately, especially through the last two lines of the first quatrain, when Cummings describes the silence of the beloved's eyes: "in your most frail gesture are things which enclose me,/ or which i cannot touch because they are too near." Thus, Cummings evokes the intense look of the beloved's speechless eyes, a look that brings color and life to the lover beyond anything perceivable in this world—even breathing life into death and ending. The lines—so simple, yet so intense—take me on a journey into love between its opening and enclosing.

The last two lines of the poem give me greatest awe when Cummings's tour de force synaesthesia becomes remarkably transformative and alive: "the voice of your eyes is deeper than all roses.../ not even the rain has such small hands." The journey is now complete, from "your eyes have their silence," to "the voice of your eyes," as if the beloved is experiencing a similar transformation, from opening to closing and enclosing, then unfolding. Who hasn't walked in the spring rain and enjoyed the light hands of its droplets? Yet, in this final quatrain, the nearness of the "voice" of the beloved's eyes touches the lover more deeply than the rain's caress.

Whenever I read this poem, I experience the enfolding and unfolding of love (in silence or in voice) and the "frail," yet "intense," gestures of love's look. For me, it communicates a deeper connection with the inner and outer world, the natural and the divine—indeed a nearest experience of "somewhere I have never traveled, gladly beyond/ any experience."

The Bustle in a House

Emily Dickinson

The Bustle in a House
The Morning after Death
Is solemnest of industries
Enacted upon Earth –

The Sweeping up the Heart
And putting Love away
We shall not want to use again
Until Eternity.

Rev. Elinor Ritchie Dalton, Ret., of Virginia Beach, writes:

This poem had never impressed me until my husband Cully's death. Six years before, I had remarried him, after being divorced eighteen years. Ours was a love affair that had no end, it seems: ups and downs, yes, but also continuity. We kept in touch because of the love we had for our son, and in retrospect, for each other.

Cully's death was not unexpected, but it was a surprise, as Death often is. That morning, I was to attend an Alzheimer's workshop. I went to the bedroom to tell Cully goodbye, only to find him lying on the floor—unresponsive. Somehow, I knew that Death had released his spirit from the body that had held his fun-loving, gentle, wise essence. I sat beside him on the floor a few minutes before I called 911, and then asked for a quiet approach.

It was after that, the real "Bustle" began. Emergency responders came, gradually filling the house. Then neighbors offered comfort and help; I told each one about Death's visit—in various words. A friend and her mother "tidied up the house." And they all talked among themselves, tacitly glad that Death had not visited their homes… yet.

Following Cully's death, I received cards and emails from family and friends. "The Bustle…" was sent by a church member, who, with his family, was more family than fellow church member. At first reading, the poem stopped me—literally "in my tracks"—as I was bustling around my house.

I cannot recall much of that day, only that the "solemnest of industries" went on; "the Sweeping up the Heart" continues to this day, "Until Eternity." And so, although I may never know what, in Emily's life, prompted her to express such deep and universal feelings about death, I am blessed by her heartfelt, forever current words.

A Valediction: Forbidding Mourning

John Donne

As virtuous men pass mildly away,
    And whisper to their souls to go,
Whilst some of their sad friends do say,
    "The breath goes now," and some say, "No,"

So let us melt, and make no noise,
    No tear-floods, nor sigh-tempests move;
'Twere profanation of our joys
    To tell the laity our love.

Moving of the earth brings harms and fears,
    Men reckon what it did and meant;
But trepidation of the spheres,
    Though greater far, is innocent.

Dull sublunary lovers' love
    (Whose soul is sense) cannot admit
Absence, because it doth remove
    Those things which elemented it.

But we, by a love so much refined
    That our selves know not what it is,
Inter-assured of the mind,
    Care less, eyes, lips, and hands to miss.

Our two souls therefore, which are one,
    Though I must go, endure not yet
A breach, but an expansion.
    Like gold to airy thinness beat.

If they be two, they are two so
    As stiff twin compasses are two:

Thy soul, the fixed foot, makes no show
　　To move, but doth, if the other do;

And though it in the center sit,
　　Yet when the other far doth roam,
It leans, and hearkens after it,
　　And grows erect, as that comes home.

Such wilt thou be to me, who must,
　　Like the other foot, obliquely run;
Thy firmness makes my circle just,
　　And makes me end where I begun.

⋖⋖⋖

Angela B. German, of Virginia Beach, writes:

I was a high school senior, enjoying life and relishing my first love, and not much else caught my attention — until my favorite teacher exposed me to what would become my passion and my career. As we read John Donne's "A Valediction: Forbidding Mourning," Donne's images of the "dull sublunary lovers" spoke to me, and I became certain of both the beauty and power of language. Donne's words directed me, and I knew I would be not only an English major but a teacher as well.

The second time I connected with this poem was in my sophomore year in college. Although I was thrilled to tackle the poem with my brilliant and somewhat intimidating professor, I quickly realized there was much more to Donne and this poem than my seventeen-year-old self previously assumed. I began to grapple with the complexity of the metaphors, and the "stiff twin compasses" came to life for me.

As an English teacher, I knew, without a doubt, that I would include Donne's "A Valediction…" in my wedding ceremony. "Two souls" now shared this love of literature and of Donne's powerful and emotive language. When starting our life together, it seemed right — for both of us — to promise that, through the years, we would continue to "lean, and [hearken] after" each other, always hoping to "[come] home."

Every year, every day that I spend in a classroom, I share my passion with a new crop of future-makers, hoping that they, too, will find literature and a passion to be "near."

The Love Song of J. Alfred Prufrock
(an excerpt)

T. S. Eliot

Let us go then, you and I,
When the evening is spread out against the sky
Like a patient etherized upon a table;
Let us go, through certain half-deserted streets,
The muttering retreats
Of restless nights in one-night cheap hotels
And sawdust restaurants with oyster-shells:
Streets that follow like a tedious argument
Of insidious intent
To lead you to an overwhelming question....
Oh, do not ask, "What is it?"
Let us go and make our visit.

In the room the women come and go
Talking of Michelangelo.

The yellow fog that rubs its back upon the window-panes,
The yellow smoke that rubs its muzzle on the window-panes
Licked its tongue into the corners of the evening,
Lingered upon the pools that stand in drains,
Let fall upon its back the soot that falls from chimneys,
Slipped by the terrace, made a sudden leap,
And seeing that it was a soft October night,
Curled once about the house, and fell asleep.

≈≈≈

Doris C. Baker, of Virginia Beach, writes:

During the Great Depression, farm children went to rural schools where they learned about vowels and punctuation in English classes. I was one of those children and later had the good fortune to be in a college literature class using the book CHIEF MODERN POETS OF ENGLAND AND AMERICA, published in 1938. That magic period of poetry still follows me after more than seventy years.

One special poem took me on strange journeys and might be the reason I chose a lifetime of travel in faraway countries. Curiosity? Sometimes even danger. Why am I still fascinated by "The Love Song of J. Alfred Prufrock?" Lately I discovered it was written in 1917, the year of my birth. And T.S. Eliot's birthday is always only one day later than mine on September calendars.

The reasons for my choice must include Eliot's natural rhythm of words, the story line or lack of one, and the poem's mysterious hidden streets and thoughts, many foreign to my experience. But also they touch the margins of my own life, bringing back forgotten possibilities, the sorrows and pleasures that enrich the memories of old age.

An Etching

Ralph Stillman Emerson

One day, long ago, my heart
Was lightly scratched by Cupid's dart.

It took so little time before
The lines were graven deep and sore.

"But Love," I cried, "is worth the price
Of pain and tears and sacrifice."

Then shadows fell. Like cruel, black crows.
They tore the petals from my rose.

Now, often as I sit alone,
I trace the etching in the stone.

৵৵৵

Kristy Feltenberger Gillespie, of Warrenton, writes:

I was born in Johnstown, Pennsylvania, best known for its Great Flood of 1889 and once bustling coal-mining industry. When I was three years old, my parents relocated to Everett, Massachusetts, a working-class suburb of Boston. My father worked in construction. My mother cared for the elderly, and my brother and I often tagged along.

Ralph Stillman Emerson was born in 1907 in Chelsea, Massachusetts. In 1908, his parents lost their home in the Great Fire and moved to Everett. Emerson wrote several poetry collections, including APPLES AND ACORNS. When my mother brought home a signed copy, she immediately handed it to me. Even at age ten, I loved words.

In the summer of 1989, my mother, brother, and I left Everett and my father for good, but she was the only one who knew this. We thought we were visiting our grandparents in Johnstown for a typical two-week trip. I realized we weren't returning when I was enrolled in the fifth grade and registered for catechism classes.

Even though my father was abusive and struggled with alcohol addiction, he was my father, and his absence felt like a death. I coped by burying myself in mountains of books which included APPLES AND ACORNS. For show and tell, most classmates brought in their Teddy Ruxpin bears or G. I. Joe toys, whereas I recited "An Etching."

To this day, this simple yet elegant poem resonates with me, and every once in a while, "I trace the etching in the stone."

Empathy

Terri Kirby Erickson

Close as two women crooning into the same
microphone, they sing their sorrows

to one another in a grocery store parking lot,
keys dangling from their hands, cars waiting

still and silent as good dogs, beside them.
People pass by unnoticed; the sky grows dark.

On and on they stand, rooted to the pavement—
sharing sadness like a loaf of warm bread—

eyes luminous as pearls formed by her friend's
suffering. Perhaps the stars will wish on them

tonight. For even as they part, briefly
touching, their glow is brighter—the ground

lit beneath their feet as they walk away,
each wearing the other woman's shoes.

Felicia Mitchell, of Meadowview, writes:

Poetry can offer sustenance. Different words resonate at different times, and thus I have a hefty mental bookshelf of poems to turn to. Sometimes I pick up Albert Huffstickler's "The Cure." In the year I lost a dear friend, my mother, and my dog, and was also diagnosed with cancer, I read "The Cure" to ground myself. "Wisdom is seeing the shape of your life," Huffstickler writes, "without obliterating (getting over) a single instant." Huffstickler's advice is good, but it was not enough during my difficult year. I needed help to see the shape of my life.

For that reason, Erickson's "Empathy" found its way onto my mental bookshelf during my experience with cancer. It spoke to me and reminded me that it is easier to see the shape of a life when friends, kindred spirits, listen to us and share their stories with us in return. In fact, during challenging times, I find myself open to having meaningful conversations in unexpected places with both dear friends and strangers who sometimes turn into friends.

When people share their lives, including their sorrows, something magical happens, I think, as Erickson's narrative illustrates. Reading the poem, I am reminded time and again that I am not alone, no matter what happens, as long as I am wise enough to treasure serendipitous gifts of empathy along with accepting what life gives me. "Sharing sadness like a loaf of warm bread" is good for the soul. Sharing sadness can lead to sharing joys.

Little Boy Blue

Eugene Field

The little toy dog is covered with dust,
　　But sturdy and staunch he stands;
And the little toy soldier is red with rust,
　　And his musket moulds in his hands.
Time was when the little toy dog was new,
　　And the soldier was passing fair;
And that was the time when our Little Boy Blue
　　Kissed them and put them there.

"Now, don't you go till I come," he said,
　　"And don't you make any noise!"
So, toddling off to his trundle-bed,
　　He dreamt of the pretty toys;
And, as he was dreaming, an angel song
　　Awakened our Little Boy Blue—
Oh! the years are many, the years are long,
　　But the little toy friends are true!

Ay, faithful to Little Boy Blue they stand,
　　Each in the same old place—
Awaiting the touch of a little hand,
　　The smile of a little face;
And they wonder, as waiting the long years through
　　In the dust of that little chair,
What has become of our Little Boy Blue,
　　Since he kissed them and put them there.

ক৸ক৸ক৸

Clay Harrison, of Williamsburg, writes:

As a typical sixteen-year-old in 1954, I had little time for poetry, until I took an advanced English class at Jefferson High School in Tampa, Florida. The teacher, Mrs. Ethel Schilling, was a no-nonsense disciplinarian. Students trembled when they passed her in the halls. Very few earned an A in her class.

Under Mrs. Schilling, we were forced to memorize poems from the masters—Poe, Frost, Longfellow— but few paid much attention, until the day she read Eugene Field's poem "Little Boy Blue" in class. The poem is about the death of a child, and as she was reading, tears flowed from her eyes. It was an awakening for me. Suddenly I realized how powerful a poem could be, to move a hard-nosed teacher like Mrs. Schilling to tears. Little did I know, at that moment, that a divine intervention had occurred in my life.

I was an only child, but my mother babysat for a neighbor who ran a print shop. The child, Lorraine Garcia, was like a sister to me. Sadly, Lorraine developed cirrhosis of the liver and passed away shortly after her second birthday. Her death broke my heart. With the words of "Little Boy Blue" imbedded in my mind, I wrote my first poem, "Little Lorraine." Her parents printed it and handed it out at the funeral.

This would the first of many poems about death that I would write over the next fifty-eight years. As a soldier during the Vietnam War and as chaplain of the Fraternal Order of Police in Tampa, I paid tribute to the fallen with a poem. In my church I still honor those who pass away with "celebration of life" poems. On every occasion, I am reminded of Mrs. Schilling standing there in the classroom, tears flowing from her eyes, reading "Little Boy Blue," and I am ever so grateful.

Dust of Snow

Robert Frost

The way a crow
Shook down on me
The dust of snow
From a hemlock tree

Has given my heart
A change of mood
And saved some part
Of a day I had rued.

Judith Stevens, of Norfolk, writes:

I have always loved this poem for its shy reminder that we immerse ourselves in nature in order to see more clearly. Spend time watching a bird build its nest, feed its young, or protect its territory: straightforward processes that have no subterfuge or double-entendre. A bird does not need any.

People are vastly more complicated than animals. The world of humans contains layers of deception, cynicism, and posturing that any self-respecting animal would disdain. Perhaps that is why this small poem, simplistic at first gaze, is so effective. The author is able to highlight a tiny incident in his day and describe in eight lines something intrinsic to human understanding: we do not know if birds have moods (do they awaken on some mornings, disinclined to sing?), but we know that humans do. Too often, we are captive to our moods, feelings that, if entertained repeatedly, can ruin a day, a relationship, sometimes a life.

Here the poet reminds us that the natural world is as close to us as we would let it in, and that nature—like the playful crow—has the power to transform us from mechanical robots into thinking, feeling human beings with an unlimited capacity for joy.

Reluctance

Robert Frost

Out through the fields and the woods
   And over the walls I have wended;
I have climbed the hills of view
   And looked at the world, and descended;
I have come by the highway home,
   And lo, it is ended.

The leaves are all dead on the ground,
   Save those that the oak is keeping
To ravel them one by one
   And let them go scraping and creeping
Out over the crusted snow,
   When others are sleeping.

And the dead leaves lie huddled and still,
   No longer blown hither and thither;
The last lone aster is gone;
   The flowers of the witch hazel wither;
The heart is still aching to seek,
   But the feet question 'Whither?'

Ah, when to the heart of man
   Was it ever less than a treason
To go with the drift of things,
   To yield with a grace to reason,
And bow and accept the end
   Of a love or a season?

❧❧❧

Jack Callan, of Norfolk, writes:

"Lo, it is ended."
        Powerful words from a walk in the woods. Something sacred, deep within, speaks to us of the retreat of sap, an oak, its keeping. We might not say it that way, but we do know it. And are those leaves really dead with their jitterbug jive of scrape and creeping — that crunch of snow after sleeping? Let's see....

"Whither?"
        Yes, lead on, we'll take this walk and risk each matter that leads to heart. And when we cannot go or yield or bow, we can love this love, this season. But do we yield with grace to reason?
        I think we take it on the chin, reluctantly.

Sermons We See

Edgar Guest

I'd rather see a sermon
than hear one any day;
I'd rather one should walk with me
than merely tell the way.
The eye's a better pupil
and more willing than the ear,
Fine counsel is confusing,
but example's always clear;
And the best of all preachers
are the men who live their creeds,
For to see good put in action
is what everybody needs.

I soon can learn to do it
if you'll let me see it done;
I can watch your hands in action,
but your tongue too fast may run.
And the lecture you deliver
may be very wise and true,
But I'd rather get my lessons
by observing what you do;
For I might misunderstand you
and the high advice you give,
But there's no misunderstanding
how you act and how you live.

Shirley Walker Moseley, of Newport News, writes:

This poem was found in my father's weathered wallet after he passed away in 1976, at age sixty-four. Obviously he had carried it for many years, as it was wrinkled, torn, and barely readable.

At age twenty-nine, in 1941, my father left the lumber mill in Pittsylvania County and came to Newport News to begin training as a welder in the Shipyard. He also left a wife and newborn baby and saw little of them over the next year. He was a rather humble man and chose throughout all his years to concentrate on just enjoying life and helping others, to the best of his ability. Throughout the short period of time that he was our Daddy, and for years after that, we heard stories from others about his deeds of kindness. (Never did we hear about them from him, and as children we were totally unaware of what he did "in secret.") No acknowledgment was necessary for him to feel appreciated, though we suspect he heard the words "thank you" many times.

When he passed away we began to realize what an exceptional man my father was. A neighbor told us of a time when he had lost his job, and with little means to support his own family of five, my father brought bags of groceries over to help him out. We observed his sacrifices as he struggled to put his girls through college, support a wife who did not work outside the home, and somehow managed to provide for the necessities of life—all on a welder's income. He also managed to sneak a few dollars into the pockets of my grandmother's apron when he visited the old home place, near Danville.

We, his three daughters, have many treasured memories of our youth; the ones that are most meaningful to us today are the examples established long ago by the hard-working, kind and humble, generous man we called "Daddy."

Abstractions from a Life in the Body

Cathryn Hankla

Any body can turn into a painted landscape
or a page in a book. Flat planes are always
ready to erase our dimensions,

as when we write half a truth and call it fiction.

The amount unknown, the vast interior,
molten core and a million facts—
the man is lying on his back in a hospital bed.

Hourly, the X-ray machine hovers over his chest.
Soon the sheet will cover his head.
For now, he is breathing.

For now, I call him "father."
In a few days his hand
Will draw away, his eyes will dull on a point

I cannot follow.

✤✤✤

May-Lily Lee, of Richmond, writes:

It's hard to imagine a travail worse than the death of a loved one. Your life changes in unimaginable ways. It makes you want to linger in the Denial phase of the Kübler-Ross model forever.

I've been journal-writing most of my life, but after my parents' deaths, I couldn't pick up a pen. Even today I don't have the right words. That's why the discovery of a poem reflecting your experience is like discovering gold sliding down the sluice. You've connected with another being who can articulate what you can't.

Besides being known for her precise language, Cathryn Hankla possesses originality of thought and insight that shines a light for the reader, and in this case a penetrating light clicked on when I read her book of poetry LAST EXPOSURES: A SEQUENCE OF POEMS. The focal point of the collection is the death of her father. I came to learn that the poet lost her father the same year I lost my mother, which makes the work resonate all the more. This poem, which reads like a sutra, exemplifies her gift and my desire to express such profound loss, and provides a meditation on transcendence and immanence.

Those Winter Sundays

Robert Hayden

Sundays too my father got up early
and put his clothes on in the blueblack cold,
then with cracked hands that ached
from labor in the weekday weather made
banked fires blaze. No one ever thanked him.

I'd wake and hear the cold splintering, breaking.
When the rooms were warm, he'd call,
and slowly I would rise and dress,
fearing the chronic angers of that house,

Speaking indifferently to him,
who had driven out the cold
and polished my good shoes as well.
What did I know, what did I know
of love's austere and lonely offices?

Maureen Theresa O'Dea, of Alexandria, writes:

I chose Robert Hayden's "Those Winter Sundays" as my nearest poem because it reminds me of growing up in Queens and seeing my father walking out the kitchen door in his black winter coat. I only saw him leave on Sunday mornings after Mass or on special occasions like Christmas Day. Every other morning, he was gone to work before all of us six children were ready to go to school. Ten years after arriving from County Clare, Ireland, he and his partner Chris Canning opened The Airline Club, and then other bars in Queens; he worked the day shift six days a week.

"Those Winter Sundays" is my nearest poem because it contrasts a child's perspective with the view of an adult who looks back and truly appreciates the details of daily work, like polishing shoes and keeping a warm house — the silent and often unrecognized forces that shape lives.

"Cracked hands," manual labor, and starting a fire: these also evoke in me images of grandparents and uncles in Ireland. I imagine them stoking a fire in the hearth stove before a day of thrashing hay in the fields. The poem opens up a world of insight into a heritage I never knew. My father worked hard because it was the office of love he knew as a child.

A Small-Sized Mystery

Jane Hirshfield

Leave a door open long enough,
a cat will enter.
Leave food, it will stay.
Soon, on cold nights,
you'll be saying "excuse me"
if you want to get out of your chair.
But one thing you'll never hear from a cat
is "excuse me."
Nor Einstein's famous theorem.
Nor "The quality of mercy is not strained."
In the dictionary of Cat, mercy is missing.
In this world where much is missing,
a cat fills only a cat-sized hole.
Yet your whole body turns toward it
again and again because it is there.

⤚⤚⤚

Jehan Rahim Mondal, of Great Falls, writes:

In mid-February of 2012, I fell in love with a young man who got a cat free from Craigslist. Although our time connecting was short, my gravity to him is much like the magic illustrated by my favorite contemporary poet, marrow-holding Jane Hirshfield. And so, I always turn to "A Small-Sized Mystery" when my heart loses the rhythm I found during those days holding perfect time, when everything was everything, and nothing needed more.

He told me a lot about his cat—how he was once so small he could fit him in his pocket, boarding the city bus, and how the cat went missing on one occasion, returning several days later with a bite from a dog. I never paid much attention to animals until I met him, someone so tuned into their world.

The beautiful thing about love is that when you really love someone or something, you feel there is no need for anything to change. The young man I loved wanted to be many things in order to grow up, but I believed he had everything already, as though I could mercifully see him years older without theorems or taglines.

Like a cat, who pads its way into a room leaving smooth, slow brushstrokes, someone pawed a place in my heart that will not wear away. This poem reminds me of the young man—gentle cat that knows so much—who forever brought me nearest to life with warm tangles, the shedding of moments and memories, sweet, true gifts.

Faucet

Julie Ellinger Hunt

I hear the faucet dripping
and in song it tells me to
shut my eyes so I try

a waterfall for tiny beings
or a drink that invisible
monsters devour

a subtle
drip, plop, splat
then it stops
when the wind comes
and drowns it out

but it is still there, dripping

even if it goes unheard

(reminds me of you)

Stan Galloway, of Bridgewater, writes:

In the fall of 2010, I heard Julie Ellinger Hunt at a poetry reading in Manhattan, New York. This was the first reading I had taken part in after turning my mind to the serious study of poetry. I had plenty of confidence issues in my own work and when I heard her read, a new calmness settled over me: a confidence, an encouragement. Her poem "Faucet" reminds me that it is not always the great gush of famous people's words that matters most but the steady and earnest voice of someone who keeps on speaking, even when no one can hear. I carry that admonition with me now.

Mother

Nagase Kiyoko
Translated by Kenneth Rexroth and Ikuko Atsumi

I am always aware of my mother,
ominous, threatening,
a pain in the depths of my consciousness.
My mother is like a shell,
so easily broken.
Yet the fact that I was born
bearing my mother's shadow
cannot be changed.
She is like a cherished, bitter dream
my nerves cannot forget
even after I awake.
She prevents all freedom of movement.
If I move she quickly breaks,
and the splinters stab me.

❧❧❧

Michal Mahgerefteh, of Norfolk, writes:

My mother battled cancer for over twenty-five years; during much of that time, she lived "like a shell… broken." After years of strong medications and experimental treatments, she was no longer the mother I knew. Her body was her own, but her essence seemed lost. At times, she became rude and inconsiderate. Unbearable. As the words of the poem say, "a pain in the depths of my consciousness." Her brokenness was like "splinters" that "stab." Yet, she was still the mother that I loved as a young girl; that "cannot be changed."

My mother passed away, in agony, in February 2010. Her death-bed cries remain with me, for I "cannot forget [them] even after I awake." For this reason, for me, the mourning is not over, "she [still] prevents all freedom of movement." And in my journey through grief, I say—even today, as I write this essay—what she could not hear in her pain: Mother, I love you!

City Lights

Gerrit Komrij
Translated by John Irons

An open space of square. Night's fallen fast.
The whole day long I've walked down narrow alleys
Where dazedly I've thought about my past:
Ash, dust and sawdust - such a woeful tally.

An open space, at last. A chiming bell.
Like some old etching lies the city square,
With scores of alleys drawn into its spell.
Arch, gateway, statue - everything is there.

The gleaming marble's listlessly approached.
The moon is full - does her awaited stint.
An owl hoots. Distant barking's faintly broached.
I see my mother standing on the plinth.

Jill M. Winkowski, of Yorktown, writes:

"I see my mother standing on the plinth." The auditorium fell silent with those last words; Gerrit Komrij had just spoken them. I was sitting in a hall in the Rotterdamse Schouwberg with a healthy audience present. A balding Dutch guy with a neck scarf sat a few seats to the right of me, and a group of pedantic-looking people occupied a few seats away on the left. I was just getting to the point of understanding a few bunches of Dutch words together, so I wondered how much I would get out of this presentation. Yet, in the poem "City Lights," Komrij's language is elemental. As a consequence, I understood almost every word. And it is quite true, that when he read the last line, the "saal" was dead still. Even the white noise seemed to disappear.

This might be why. Typical Dutch architecture is made up of tall row-style buildings. To get through the residential sections of cities, you pass through narrow alleyways that may lead you to a canal with a bridge or to a square. In this poem, Komrij talks about walking down narrow alleys for an entire day, until night fell. And we know, from the last stanza, that however unplanned and seemingly unconscious this walk was for the narrator, he had done all this before.

The last line of the poem took me by surprise, and still does. All at once, the daylong walk through alleyways has become a walk through the poet's psyche. Komrij maintains the magic of the square while speaking through the voice of a poet who has walked these (inner) pathways many times. It doesn't matter which alleyway. It is familiar and it leads to the same place. To the city square. And now, to the image of the mother/statue, cold, lit up by a full moon, gleaming and untouchable.

Woodchucks

Maxine Kumin

Gassing the woodchucks didn't turn out right.
The knockout bomb from the Feed and Grain Exchange
was featured as merciful, quick at the bone
and the case we had against them was airtight,
both exits shoehorned shut with puddingstone,
but they had a sub-sub-basement out of range.

Next morning they turned up again, no worse
for the cyanide than we for our cigarettes
and state-store Scotch, all of us up to scratch.
They brought down the marigolds as a matter of course
and then took over the vegetable patch
nipping the broccoli shoots, beheading the carrots.

The food from our mouths, I said, righteously thrilling
to the feel of the .22, the bullets' neat noses.
I, a lapsed pacifist fallen from grace
puffed with Darwinian pieties for killing,
now drew a bead on the little woodchuck's face.
He died down in the everbearing roses.

Ten minutes later I dropped the mother. She
flipflopped in the air and fell, her needle teeth
still hooked in a leaf of early Swiss chard.
Another baby next. O one-two-three
the murderer inside me rose up hard,
the hawkeye killer came on stage forthwith.

There's one chuck left. Old wily fellow, he keeps
me cocked and ready day after day after day.
All night I hunt his humped-up form. I dream
I sight along the barrel in my sleep.
If only they'd all consented to die unseen
gassed underground the quiet Nazi way.

⊰⊰⊰

Sara M. Robinson, of Charlottesville, writes:

This poem, when I first met it a few years ago, struck me hard with its metaphoric qualities. What seems, on the surface, to be a simple poem about dealing with a particular farm pest, revealed itself on each subsequent reading as a major witness to a horrific event.

I come from Eastern European Jewish and German stock. I know, from stories I heard as a child and from the news as I grew up, the horrors of the Holocaust. Every nation or political group, at one time or another, has their "pests." Some manage to escape to unknown and frightening freedoms; some don't.

My relatives landed in Virginia's Shenandoah Valley and in that rural setting they became merchants of basic supplies, serving mostly farmers. I grew up with a father whose photographic hobby enabled him to record over three generations of local folks and publish nine books of these photos. His writings in these books were anecdotal, warm, and loving. His family merged into the local landscape in ways that ultimately formed me.

Late in life, I became a creative writer. First was a memoir about my well-known father and my mother, followed by my first book of poetry. My writings continuously return to a love of my home town and a deep understanding of why I am here. I want my poetry to please and disturb, as Ms. Kumin's poem does. This is what I think poetry can do: create the perspective.

The Trees

Philip Larkin

The trees are coming into leaf
Like something almost being said;
The recent buds relax and spread,
Their greenness is a kind of grief.

Is it that they are born again
And we grow old? No, they die too,
Their yearly trick of looking new
Is written down in rings of grain.

Yet still the unresting castles thresh
In fullgrown thickness every May.
Last year is dead, they seem to say,
Begin afresh, afresh, afresh.

❧❧❧

Beverly Foote, of Virginia Beach, writes:

Every spring I think of Larkin's words, "The trees are coming into leaf/…Their greenness is a kind of grief," and I ask myself the same question: why does Larkin associate the arrival of spring with grief? It would seem logical to connect grief with the barrenness of winter when nature folds in on itself and the trees, having made a magnificent display of color, yield to the natural process of dying.

In the spring of 2013, however, Larkin's poem spoke to me in a new way. I thought of my husband who had died recently. His love had always been to me the grand flourish of springtime, where once-barren trees become castles of greenery. Now each daffodil that pushed its way through the cold earth activated the pain of loss. It seemed a natural trickery that the first buds, early blossoms of dogwoods, and perky pansies were all looking new while my heart was so heavy.

Even today, in moments of grief, Larkin's poem reminds me that death is a part of life, and although loss makes change poignant, there remains hope for renewal. Nature speaks tenderly to that grief in the soft sound of leaves on a late spring night, urging acceptance of life in its fullness with the gentle words, "Begin afresh, afresh, afresh." With my heart I listen to that soothing sibilance, and I too begin my life again.

The Highwayman

(an excerpt)

Alfred Noyes

"And still of a winter's night, they say, when the wind is in the trees,
When the moon is a ghostly galleon tossed upon cloudy seas,
When the road is a ribbon of moonlight over the purple moor,
A highwayman comes riding—
    Riding—riding—
A highwayman comes riding, up to the old inn-door.

Over the cobbles he clatters and clangs in the dark inn-yard.
He taps with his whip on the shutters, but all is locked and barred.
He whistles a tune to the window, and who should be waiting there
But the landlord's black-eyed daughter,
    Bess, the landlord's daughter,
Plaiting a dark red love-knot into her long black hair."

Naomi Rodman, of Blacksburg, writes:

My nearest poem is "The Highwayman" by Alfred Noyes. I first heard this poem in my middle school English class, read by an elderly lady who (I must reveal) expressed no real feeling or attached any meaning to it. It wasn't until a few years later in high school that I heard the poem again, this time sung by artist Loreena McKennitt. That was when the poem truly touched me.

I'm a young woman and (probably because of that) I can't help that tragic and true love speaks to me more than anything else. The repetition and the rhythm and rhyme of Noyes's poem all come together to create a beautiful description of a love story, better than any love experience in real life. My favorite stanzas of this long poem are the last two. They describe how love can transcend even death—yes, even our physical demise.

Wild Heart

for Trisha

Gregory Orr

Where would I be if not for your wild heart?
I ask this not for love, but selfishly—
how could I live? How could I make my art?
Questions I wouldn't ask if I were smart.
Take the whole thing on faith. Blind eyes can see
where would I be if not for your wild heart.
Love or need—who can tell the two apart?
Nor does it matter much, since both agree
that I need you to live and make my art.
Are you the target; am I the bow and dart?
Are you the deer that doesn't want to flee
and turns to give the hunter her wild heart?
I bite the apple and the apple's tart
but that's the complex taste of destiny.
How could I live? How could I make my art
in some bland place like Eden, set apart
from the world's tumult and its agony?
Where would I be if not for your wild heart?
How could I live? How could I make my art?

Barbara Drucker Smith, of Newport News, writes:

"Wild Heart" by Gregory Orr, my nearest poem, is from his book of poetry THE CAGED OWL, which I first encountered in 2004, at the 4th Annual Library of Virginia Awards Celebration Honoring Virginia Authors. Before leaving the library I approached Gregory Orr. His demeanor was humble, and he seemed to appreciate my complimentary comments. Needless to say, I chose his book as a going-away gift to the attendees.

I found in Orr's poetry a frank likeness to my poems, not only in content and subject matter, but also in the way the poems were configured on the page. It was this awareness that catapulted me into organizing my poems into a first book, A POETIC JOURNEY. I owe much to Gregory Orr.

Orr tells us that he, too, owes a debt, and his poem "Wild Heart" is written for Trisha, whom he clearly loves and appreciates and to whom he credits his success as a poet. "How could I live? How could I make my art?" he writes, at the poem's closing. Trisha is his inspiration and great love.

Those of us who write, who are poets, have special people who influence our ability to make our art. To a great extent, we owe them our poetry.

Their Eyes All Aglow

Sarah Dunning Park

What, I wonder,
will they remember
from their childhoods?
If everything experienced
is somehow stored—
stitched into the brain's cortical folds
like a heap of colorful rags
carefully braided and coiled
to make the rug underfoot—
which bits and pieces of memory
will present face-up,
to be felt and seen
and trod upon daily?

I would happily tinker with their minds—
to gently tuck out of reach the memories
of times I snapped at them in anger,
or to bring forward and shore up
their recollection of the days
when all was peaceful,
and love imbued every word.

But I can't control their minds
—nor mine, tonight,
as I snuff out a stub of candle
on our table, and its smoking wick
and heady scent bring on a wave
of remembering I didn't expect:
the feel of a Christmas Eve
when it's late and I am little,
full to bursting with rich food
and my wild impatience
for the morning.

৵৵৵

Martha Moruza Hepler, of Old Town Alexandria, writes:

My daughter has moved three times in her almost four years, once across town and twice across the Pacific. I think she will remember this last trip: the longest plane ride a kid can stand, on the far, dim side of which will have been an island of shimmering heat, fighter jets overhead, and a new baby brother. I have similar memories of a far-off country and a dad in a scratchy uniform who took us there. When she's grown, will good memories bubble to the surface, as they have for me? Or will it be the missing of her father while he was at war, her mother's brimming-over stress, the extreme jet lag, the loneliness for friends left behind?

We're humans raising humans, and every childhood is imperfect. "Their Eyes All Aglow" encapsulates my wish for my children's memories to brim with soft landings in a safe place. It takes my frazzled half-prayed thoughts and embodies them. It is a companion in the intensities of motherhood, my reassurance that others have fought the same fights with fierce love.

After coming across this poem online, I bought Sarah Dunning Park's collection WHAT IT IS IS BEAUTIFUL. Her poetry is about mothering her three kids, and I found she was speaking my language. My hands and brain are full these days, of good and busy little things; it is a relief to read how someone on the other side of the littlest years brings clarity and camaraderie to my current situation.

Sky Inside

Molly Peacock

To understand is to stand under the sky
Of your own desires. Instincts are always
To grow. Watch that insane boy to see why
He shakes his hands and head and never plays.
He is too busy trying to grow through
The firestorm of terror that shakes him.
People who do not see you will watch you
And tell you what you are according to them,
Self-destructive, or tortured, or any
One of the terms the mind employs to put
Itself over the matter. The many
Nodes of growth on your limbs are unseen; brute
Pressure of the sap inside you makes you grow
While the worlds inside you smoke and blow.

Cašmir Hodge, of Petersburg, writes:

The poem I have chosen as a nearest poem is "Sky Inside," a poem about addiction. Addiction, I feel, is a very serious issue and a problem that is very prominent in my family, so this poem really got to me.

The way this poem was written isn't very specific; the poet doesn't tell us what the person is addicted to, what the "firestorm of terror" is. I find that unusual, but powerful in its own way, because it creates this almost fairy-tale feeling, as if this is not real, not really happening. It is just some horrid imaginary thing floating around in someone's head. But addiction is very real and very prevalent. By not specifying the addiction in the poem, the poet allows the reader to insert nearly any addictive substance into it. The poem and its horror would still make sense.

In her poem Molly Peacock wrote, "The many/ Nodes of growth on your limbs are unseen; brute/ Pressure of the sap inside you makes you grow/ While the worlds inside you smoke and blow." This part really touched me because it gave me the sense of falling apart from the inside out, which is what happens to addicts. Addiction starts internally, it slowly decays the inside until it reaches the surface and infects others as well, so they're dragged under by their loved one with the addiction.

It surprised me that someone who's gone through this, or experienced this with someone, would put so much detail (vague but strong) and so much feeling into the writing, so that the reader gets that punch-in-the-gut feeling. I really loved this poem because I got that feeling when I read it the first time.

Matamis

Jon Pineda

One summer in Pensacola,
I held an orange this way,
flesh hiding beneath
the texture of the rind,
then slipped my thumbs
into its core & folded it
open, like a book.

When I held out the halves,
the juice seemed to trace
the veins in my arms
as it dripped down to my elbows
& darkened spots of sand.
We were sitting on the beach then,
the sun, spheres of light within each piece.
I remember thinking, in Tagalog,
the word *matamis* is sweet in English,
though I did not say it for fear
of mispronouncing the language.

Instead, I finished the fruit & offered
nothing except my silence, & my father,
who pried apart another piece, breaking
the globe in two, offered me half.
Meaning everything.

༄ ༄ ༄

Bill Glose, of Yorktown, writes:

I grew up in a house built on a foundation of silence. We didn't air our dirty secrets in public, or in private. Hurts, worries, fears: those were things to bottle up and pretend didn't exist. I never talked about them, nor did I write about them. Not until I read Jon Pineda's superb poem, "Matamis."

In the poem, a father and his adult son sit together as the son peels and splits an orange. Resentment radiates from the son, and it becomes obvious that a painful wedge of shared history has driven itself between them. The son keeps both orange halves for himself, sharing nothing with his father but silence. But in the final lines, the father makes a gesture that shows his desire to heal their wounds, leaving the reader with a sense of hope for their future.

I was struck by the way Pineda was able to talk about his hurt feelings over his father's absence without excoriating him. His poem is a beautiful vignette that delves into the strange concoction of confusion and devotion, love and frustration that makes up familial relationships. The Filipino influence prevalent in Pineda's poetry didn't dissuade me from feeling that his poem spoke to my own Irish-Catholic upbringing. His specific example beamed with universal insight.

After reading "Matamis," I sat down and wrote my own poems about family, about the deafening quiet and misunderstandings that grew out of silence. I shared them with my parents, whose reactions I braced to receive. Instead of anger, they showed me love and pride. Best of all, we finally talked.

The House at Rest

Jessica Powers

On a dark night
Kindled in love with yearnings
Oh, happy chance!
I went forth unobserved,
My house being now at rest.
        -Saint John of the Cross

How does one hush one's house,
each proud possessive wall, each sighing rafter,
the rooms made restless with remembered laughter
or wounding echoes, the permissive doors,
the stairs that vacillate from up to down,
windows that bring in color and event
from countryside or town,
oppressive ceilings and complaining floors?

The house must first of all accept the night.
Let it erase the walls and their display,
impoverish the rooms till they are filled
with humble silences; let clocks be stilled
and all the selfish urgencies of day.

Midnight is not the time to greet a guest.
Caution the doors against both foes and friends,
and try to make the windows understand
their unimportance when the daylight ends.
Persuade the stairs to patience, and deny
the passages their aimless to and fro.
Virtue it is that puts a house at rest.
How well repaid that tenant is, how blest
who, when the call is heard,
is free to take his kindled heart and go.

❧❧❧

Marie A. Barthelemy, of Williamsburg, writes:

When the call is heard, the heart is free to go and surrender to a new journey. The soul, now transformed into bread and wine, labors effortlessly toward compassion. New vistas open to a grass greener than before. The daily tasks are pieced one by one into a joyous sigh. The laundry still needs to be done, and the meals prepared. Shall I cook chicken divan or beef Stroganoff this evening? Let us light the candles, open a bottle of old Merlot, and whip Julia Child's chocolate mousse. Tonight is a celebration! Knock at the neighbors' doors and let them know they are invited to our house. Come as you are; we will share stories, laughter, and tears. At six, we will start the blessings. No ending time; we have the entire night....

The grey sobbing of missed opportunities, misunderstandings, and estrangements vanishes into a new name: that of a master cook on a mission! And it all comes to happen after a very dark night.

My Shadow

Robert Louis Stevenson

I have a little shadow that goes in and out with me,
And what can be the use of him is more than I can see.
He is very, very like me from the heels up to the head;
And I see him jump before me, when I jump into my bed.

The funniest thing about him is the way he likes to grow—
Not at all like proper children, which is always very slow;
For he sometimes shoots up taller like an india-rubber ball,
And he sometimes gets so little that there's none of him at all.

He hasn't got a notion of how children ought to play,
And can only make a fool of me in every sort of way.
He stays so close behind me, he's a coward you can see;
I'd think shame to stick to nursie as that shadow sticks to me!

One morning, very early, before the sun was up,
I rose and found the shining dew on every buttercup;
But my lazy little shadow, like an arrant sleepy-head,
Had stayed at home behind me and was fast asleep in bed.

Carolyn Kreiter-Foronda, of Hardyville, writes:

As a child, I fed my imagination by playing in the shadows of a weeping willow tree. Leaning against the trunk, I watched billowy shapes sweep the lawn as the sun marched across the sky. Late at night, after tucking me in bed, my mother read selections from Robert Louis Stevenson's classic book, A CHILD'S GARDEN OF VERSES. I can still hear the lilt in her voice as she emphasized rich rhythms and rhymes. A gifted teacher, she explained the power of similes in my favorite poem, "My Shadow," so I could envision the magical transformation of a dark image shooting "up taller like an india-rubber ball." After she left the room, I recited the stanzas from memory while watching my own shadow flit in and out of lamplight.

How fortunate I was to have a mother who chose to share memorable poetry. Her love of words ignited my desire to start writing poems at the age of four. Listening to her gentle voice as she read lyrical lines led to the fine-tuning of my ear to melodic words arranged in the right order.

Whenever I return to the foothills of my childhood, I drive by the site of the old willow tree where shadows first sparked my creativity. Although the tree no longer graces the lawn, a flood of memories fills my heart with the desire to relive those days of youth when reflections took on lives of their own, skipping across the grass like playmates.

Casey at the Bat

Ernest Lawrence Thayer ("Phin")

The Outlook wasn't brilliant for the Mudville nine that day:
The score stood four to two, with but one inning more to play.
And then when Cooney died at first, and Barrows did the same,
A sickly silence fell upon the patrons of the game.

A straggling few got up to go in deep despair. The rest
Clung to that hope which springs eternal in the human breast;
They thought, if only Casey could get but a whack at that –
We'd put up even money, now, with Casey at the bat.

But Flynn preceded Casey, as did also Jimmy Blake,
And the former was a lulu and the latter was a cake;
So upon that stricken multitude grim melancholy sat,
For there seemed but little chance of Casey's getting to the bat.

But Flynn let drive a single, to the wonderment of all,
And Blake, the much despis-ed, tore the cover off the ball;
And when the dust had lifted, and the men saw what had occurred,
There was Jimmy safe at second and Flynn a-hugging third.

Then from 5,000 throats and more there rose a lusty yell;
It rumbled through the valley, it rattled in the dell;
It knocked upon the mountain and recoiled upon the flat,
For Casey, mighty Casey, was advancing to the bat.

There was ease in Casey's manner as he stepped into his place;
There was pride in Casey's bearing and a smile on Casey's face.
And when, responding to the cheers, he lightly doffed his hat,
No stranger in the crowd could doubt 'twas Casey at the bat.

Ten thousand eyes were on him as he rubbed his hands with dirt;
Five thousand tongues applauded when he wiped them on his shirt.
Then while the writhing pitcher ground the ball into his hip,
Defiance gleamed in Casey's eye, a sneer curled Casey's lip.

And now the leather-covered sphere came hurtling through the air,
And Casey stood a-watching it in haughty grandeur there.
Close by the sturdy batsman the ball unheeded sped –
"That ain't my style," said Casey. "Strike one," the umpire said.

From the benches, black with people, there went up a muffled roar,
Like the beating of the storm-waves on a stern and distant shore.
"Kill him! Kill the umpire!" shouted someone on the stand;
And it's likely they'd a-killed him had not Casey raised his hand.

With a smile of Christian charity great Casey's visage shone;
He stilled the rising tumult; he bade the game go on;
He signaled to the pitcher, and once more the spheroid flew;
But Casey still ignored it, and the umpire said, "Strike two."

"Fraud!" cried the maddened thousands, and echo answered fraud;
But one scornful look from Casey and the audience was awed.
They saw his face grow stern and cold, they saw his muscles strain,
And they knew that Casey wouldn't let that ball go by again.

The sneer is gone from Casey's lip, his teeth are clenched in hate;
He pounds with cruel violence his bat upon the plate.
And now the pitcher holds the ball, and now he lets it go,
And now the air is shattered by the force of Casey's blow.

Oh, somewhere in this favored land the sun is shining bright;
The band is playing somewhere, and somewhere hearts are light,
And somewhere men are laughing, and somewhere children shout
But there is no joy in Mudville – mighty Casey has struck out.

❧❧❧

Solomon McCray, III, of James City County, writes:

I choose "Casey at the Bat" by Ernest Thayer as my nearest poem because it is a classic. Baseball is a game of tradition, and this poem has been passed down from generation to generation. It brings out the early days of baseball, when it was young and people from all over flocked to the games. It truly shows how it is America's pastime.

The poem also brings out a sense of competition in me. The fact that there are so many people at the game makes me think of it as a cross-town rivalry. And I feel I could be Casey, except that I wouldn't want to have the same fate he had!

Memories frequently come up when I read this poem. I remember a time when I was in the pitcher's shoes, but instead of being able to get the batter out, he got a hit off me to win the game. Then there was the time I was in Casey's shoes. After a long battle I had worked the count full. With butterflies in my stomach and what felt like the weight of the world on me, I got the game-winning hit to left field. As a baseball player myself, I believe that every baseball fan or player should appreciate the story of Casey and the Mudville nine.

To Kiss a Forehead

Marina Tsvetaeva
Translated by Ilya Kaminsky and Jean Valentine

To kiss a forehead is to erase worry.
I kiss your forehead.

To kiss the eyes is to lift sleeplessness.
I kiss your eyes.

To kiss the lips is to drink water.
I kiss your lips.

To kiss a forehead is to erase memory.
I kiss your forehead.

Deborah Mallett Spanich, of Lynchburg, writes:

I became very attached to my father in my infancy. While my mother suffered severe postpartum depression, he walked the floors with me at nights. He wasn't perfect, although that's how I saw him as a child. He was a man who lived with losses and sadness, a sense of unworthiness and failure, and an inability to let go of the past. I realized as I grew older that he'd given up early on. He believed that, like his parents, he wouldn't have a long life. The truth is, it was more of a death wish.

I was twenty-seven when my father died after a stroke at age fifty-one. I stood by the hospital bed with my sisters like bookends beside me. It was the first time I had ever seen a dead body. I put my hand on my father's head, where the lines I recognized so well crossed the span above his brows. His skin was already less warm than when I had last touched him. I was almost overwhelmed. I felt as if I were saying goodbye to my own child. I whispered, "It's all right. It's okay." I leaned over and kissed his forehead.

Sometime in the next few weeks I came across the Tsvetaeva poem "To Kiss a Forehead." When I read it, the moment of kissing my father came back. I cried, because I had lost him, and because I wished I could have kissed his forehead sooner.

Love after Love

Derek Walcott

The time will come
when, with elation
you will greet yourself arriving
at your own door, in your own mirror
and each will smile at the other's welcome,

and say, sit here. Eat.
You will love again the stranger who was your self.
Give wine. Give bread. Give back your heart
to itself, to the stranger who has loved you

all your life, whom you ignored
for another, who knows you by heart.
Take down the love letters from the bookshelf,

the photographs, the desperate notes,
peel your own image from the mirror.
Sit. Feast on your life.

Ann McDowell, of Virginia Beach, writes:

Derek Walcott's "Love after Love" captured me the first time I heard it read at a conference years ago. I still don't understand it entirely, but this only makes the poem all the more intriguing. My appreciation borders on the ineffable; I never tire of the poem's mystery.

In a Quote Book I keep, Walcott's poem is grouped with a Henry Miller quote that ends "... and we shall know ourselves for the first time" and with T.S. Eliot's "and the end of all our exploring will be to arrive where we started and know the place for the first time." This finding ourselves at home, after searching all over the world, seems a recurrent theme for writers. Walcott's poem is a passionate expression of this idea; it portrays both a welcome and an awakening: an epiphany.

Many of us spend our lives searching for acceptance and love or approval from others, perhaps from those who didn't love us enough in our childhood, and we wander about with a hole in our hearts crying to be filled. Unable to fill our emptiness with shiny possessions, we may even pretend to be someone we aren't. As Walcott suggests, "the stranger who was your self."

But somehow, with luck or wisdom, this "stranger who has loved you/ all your life, whom you ignored/ for another...." — your own true self — will at last be recognized as the one who can give you the love and acceptance you crave. It is a joyous reunion.

I don't believe we can love others unless we are able to love ourselves. Derek Walcott seems to be celebrating this idea "with elation." If we reach this desired state, we can then feast on our lives, knowing ourselves for the first time.

Elephant Grave

Victoria White

After an elephant dies,
the herd may carry its bones for miles.
Did you know that? Hefting them over
the flatland ebb and flow, as

years ago we trekked
the backwoods of late November,
New England burned out like candlewick.
White light parted maples then,
found me chasing your footsteps
as you led us home.
Last fall the hills blazed red—?
I wonder if you tasted smoke, oceans away
as the first shells hit and
you couldn't run.
Did you think of the leaves
we used to bring home and tape up,
the way they all withered in the end?
Even the best, the brightest
come to nothing, I learned,

because there wasn't a body
even though you promised to come back.
I broke when I heard you were lying
alone in scrub grass,
no one to lift you up, knowing
you were precious.
Brother, I would have carried you
on my shoulders 'til the horizon bent for us
and our forest dawned along its edge.
Imagine, and the maples stoop to greet you,
saying welcome back,
welcome home.

～❦～

Nathan Salle, of Richmond, writes:

The poem "Elephant Grave" was the 2012 first prize winner of the Patricia Grodd Poetry Prize for Young Writers competition held by the KENYON REVIEW. In my Poetry I class we were required to submit to the contest, and while reviewing the contest guidelines, I decided to read the poems by the past winners and so discovered this poem. I'm sure glad I found it.

Generally the poems I read don't leave me with a notable feeling or have a lasting effect. Perhaps the only other poem out there that I've read that has stuck with me is "Casey at the Bat" by Ernest Thayer. There is something about this poem, though, that really reaches me. Each time I read it, I feel a huge sense of urgency to go help someone, to go help my sister, to go help the brother I don't even have. I love the way this poem progresses, and the opening stanza with the elephants is fantastic — you can see the herd walking for miles, carrying the bones of the dead elephant. Not only is that section great, but the way the poem flows, making a transition from idea to idea, is, in my view, flawless. Not once was I confused about where I was. I was so captured by the images that I could see myself in the African plains carrying my best friend to safety, and the poem made me want to be the hero. It's dreadfully sad too: a soldier lost at war, never to return home.

I would never want to have to experience the pain the narrator had to go through; yet, I would call "Elephant Grave" my nearest poem because this is the kind of poem that I would like to write.

The Lake Isle of Innisfree

William Butler Yeats

I will arise and go now, and go to Innisfree,
And a small cabin build there, of clay and wattles made:
Nine bean-rows will I have there, a hive for the honey-bee,
And live alone in the bee-loud glade.

And I shall have some peace there, for peace comes dropping slow,
Dropping from the veils of the morning to where the cricket sings;
There midnight's all a glimmer, and noon a purple glow,
And evening full of the linnet's wings.

I will arise and go now, for always night and day
I hear lake water lapping with low sounds by the shore;
While I stand on the roadway, or on the pavements grey,
I hear it in the deep heart's core.

Cynthia Johnson Newlon, of Wise, writes:

"I hear lake water lapping with low sounds by the shore." This line takes me to a place — my place — the home place of my family. Hot afternoons and evenings swinging on my Aunt Beulah's front porch, listening to the gurgle of the brook along the front yard: here, I always felt peace; always felt home. Like Yeats, who spent much of his time away from Sligo County, Ireland, I have gone, in my mind, to my Innisfree. There, in the home of Aunt Beulah, I found a constant in life. And I connect her and the home place as one.

Aunt Beulah, my dad's only sister, lived in the family home nearly until her death at the age of ninety-seven. It was an old two-story farmhouse, on three-and-a-half acres of land, bordered on the north side by a large creek and on the south side by Highway 58.

My best memories of my "Innisfree" are of summer visits, mornings spent helping Aunt Beulah in her small garden out back or weeding the front flower beds. From her front porch, there were also shrubs and blooming trees to behold. The smell of the apple tree remains vividly in my senses; the taste of Aunt Beulah's fried apples is seared on my palate. In the evenings, lightning bugs lit up the front lawn, a show unrivaled by any man-made spectacle. These memories are my "bee-loud glade," and I hold them and Aunt Beulah in my heart.

Aunt Beulah is gone now and so is my sense of place. For the last twenty-five years, she was my mother, and her home was my home. Nevertheless, "for always night and day" I have my own virtual Innisfree, to arise and go and "have some peace there." I cling to it and will cling to it, for as long as I stand alone on my own roadway.

Meaning

For it is important that awake people be awake,
or a breaking line may discourage them back to sleep;
the signals we give—yes or no, or maybe—
should be clear: the darkness around us is deep.

William Stafford, the poet

The island of light that grows
with expanding consciousness
and genuine connectedness
is our only hope.

Thayer Cory, the reader

Variations on the Word Love

Margaret Atwood

This is a word we use to plug
holes with. It's the right size for those warm
blanks in speech, for those red heart-
shaped vacancies on the page that look nothing
like real hearts. Add lace
and you can sell
it. We insert it also in the one empty
space on the printed form
that comes with no instructions. There are whole
magazines with not much in them
but the word love, you can
rub it all over your body and you
can cook with it too. How do we know
it isn't what goes on at the cool
debaucheries of slugs under damp
pieces of cardboard? As for the weed-
seedlings nosing their tough snouts up
among the lettuces, they shout it.
Love! Love! sing the soldiers, raising
their glittering knives in salute.

Then there's the two
of us. This word
is far too short for us, it has only
four letters, too sparse
to fill those deep bare
vacuums between the stars
that press on us with their deafness.

It's not love we don't wish
to fall into, but that fear
this word is not enough but it will
have to do. It's a single
vowel in this metallic
silence, a mouth that says
O again and again in wonder
and pain, a breath, a finger
grip on a cliffside. You can
hold on or let go.

Joan C. Meyer, of Vienna, writes:

When I first read "Variations on the Word Love" my response was "a single vowel," somewhat sexual in release, and relief of recognition and resonance. Later, working on this essay in the silver light and "metallic silence" of my laptop's screen, I was still only "a mouth that says/ O again and again in wonder/ and pain," in answer to the poem.

The poet Margaret Atwood seems to share my fetish for linguistics as well as a fascination with the limitations and failures of language. Atwood once commented that Inuits in the northern climes have numerous words for "white." Her comments addressed also a common misconception, for they do have numerous words for "snow," in its various circumstances. As in German, Inuit nouns are building blocks whose modifying affixes are added, sequentially, leading to words like "tuntussuqatarniksaitengqiggtuq," a thirty-letter word (the longest in the Inuit language) meaning "He had not yet said again that he was going to hunt reindeer."

Anglos do not have a whole variety of words to articulate love accurately. And although we address this by tacking on conditional prefaces such as "platonic" or "romantic," which serve as prefixes in casual and serious usage alike, "This word/ is far too short for us, it has only/ four letters, too sparse/ to fill those deep bare/ vacuums between the stars/ that press on us with their deafness." This is why poetry itself is so important and why I love it so much. Poetry—certainly, this poem—conveys the complexity of the human condition and expresses the emotions we have in a way that a single word, no matter the length, in any language at all, never could.

Heaven on Earth

Kristin Berkey-Abbott

I saw Jesus at the bowling alley,
slinging nothing but gutter balls.
He said, "You've gotta love a hobby
that allows ugly shoes."
He lit a cigarette and bought me a beer
So I invited him to dinner.

I knew the Lord couldn't see my house
in its current condition, so I gave it an out
of season spring cleaning. What to serve
for dinner? Fish—the logical
choice, but after 2000 years, he must grow weary
of everyone's favorite seafood dishes.
I thought of my Granny's ham with Coca Cola
glaze, but you can't serve that to a Jewish
boy. Likewize pizza—all my favorite
toppings involve pork.

In the end, I made us an all-dessert buffet.
We played Scrabble and Uno and Yahtzee
and listened to Bill Monroe.
Jesus has a healthy appetite for sweets,
I'm happy to report. He told strange
stories which I've puzzled over for days now.

We've got an appointment for golf on Wednesday.
Ordinarily I don't play, and certainly not in this humidity.
But the Lord says he knows a grand miniature
golf course with fiberglass mermaids and working windmills
and the best homemade ice cream you ever tasted.
Sounds like heaven to me.

ॐ ॐ ॐ

Tom Berkey, of Williamsburg, writes:

I've selected "Heaven on Earth," a poem by Kristin Berkey-Abbott, to be my nearest poem, because few poems expose my prejudices as this poem does every time read it. With a wallop, heaven and earth change places; heaven becomes commonplace and earthly existence heavenly.

The poem poses the possibility that strangers we meet in this life might be Jesus in disguise. What is striking is that Jesus and the bowler are doing the common things that make up our mundane daily lives. Jesus is a regular guy, having a smoke and a beer. He's probably wearing jeans and a sweatshirt. What? No robe, sandals, or beard? If these two characters were really religious people, I would expect they would be doing what I consider to be "religious" activities such as helping the poor. Instead, they're having a good time doing things I like to do, and, like me, apparently not thinking too much about the poor of this world. Or are they? We get a hint that Jesus was doing exactly the provocative ministry he's known for in the Bible when the poet says, "He told strange stories...."

I like the poet's direct and uncluttered style reminiscent of Billy Collins. The words may be spare, but the imagery they create is rich with meaning. I identify instantly with the bowler, especially getting ready for the visit of a celebrity. Except for the contemporary situation, the poem's theme is ageless — the antithesis of the common person doing common activities, offering hospitality to the unknown stranger who, in this case, turns out to be none other than God.

A Poison Tree

William Blake

I was angry with my friend:
I told my wrath, my wrath did end.
I was angry with my foe:
I told it not, my wrath did grow.

And I watered it in fears,
Night and morning with my tears;
And I sunned it with smiles,
And with soft deceitful wiles.

And it grew both day and night,
Till it bore an apple bright,
And my foe beheld it shine,
And he knew that it was mine,

And into my garden stole
When the night had veiled the pole;
In the morning, glad, I see
My foe outstretched beneath the tree.

Tristan Rose, of Clintwood, writes:

I first encountered Blake along with this poem when I was in high school over fifteen years ago. Although I knew very little of Blake when I first read the poem, it resonated and stuck with me. I was especially attuned to the idea of retribution and strange karma that the poem seemed to present. When I attended college (the first time around, I am an older student now) and learned even more about Blake, I started to appreciate this poem for more reasons.

The poem is one of the few by Blake that is somewhat dark and seems to go against the celebration of God and religion that encompasses a majority of his poems. Since then, I have identified strongly with this poem because of the message that I interpret from it. I see this poem as a reminder that, even though we may do our best and live a large percentage of our lives in accordance with our definition of what is good/righteous/moral, there always exists a part of us that hungers for the darkness. Be it vengeance disguised as justice or violence performed in the name of good, mankind and individual alike must be aware of and vigilant toward this dark side, which can rise up even within the best and most devout among us.

Falling far short of most devout or righteous, I use this poem to remind myself to be vigilant against the darkness that all too often finds a seemingly justifiable excuse to rear its ugly head.

Jabberwocky

Lewis Carroll

'Twas brillig, and the slithy toves
Did gyre and gimble in the wabe:
All mimsy were the borogoves,
And the mome raths outgrabe.

"Beware the Jabberwock, my son!
The jaws that bite, the claws that catch!
Beware the Jubjub bird, and shun
The frumious Bandersnatch!"

He took his vorpal sword in hand:
Long time the manxome foe he sought –
So rested he by the Tumtum tree,
And stood awhile in thought.

And, as in uffish thought he stood,
The Jabberwock, with eyes of flame,
Came whiffling through the tulgey wood,
And burbled as it came!

One, two! One, two! And through and through
The vorpal blade went snicker-snack!
He left it dead, and with its head
He went galumphing back.

"And, has thou slain the Jabberwock?
Come to my arms, my beamish boy!
O frabjous day! Callooh! Callay!"
He chortled in his joy.

'Twas brillig, and the slithy toves
Did gyre and gimble in the wabe;
All mimsy were the borogoves,
And the mome raths outgrabe.

᪥᪥᪥

Wendy R. Blair, of Roanoke, writes:

> *"When I use a word," Humpty Dumpty said, in rather a scornful tone,*
> *"it means just what I choose it to mean—neither more nor less."*
> *THROUGH THE LOOKING GLASS AND*
> *WHAT ALICE FOUND THERE*
> *—Lewis Carroll (1871)*

We were a family of readers. I was Little Jack Hornered and mittenless kittened from infancy, nursery rhymes requiring nothing of the reader but a giggle or two. So when my father first recited "Jabberwocky," I had no frame of reference. It confused and enchanted. Beyond the nonsense, secrets clamored to be revealed. A real poem.

That evening, as I nestled in my father's lap, he and Mr. Carroll taught me to use my "uffish" imagination, how poetry could, and should, evoke emotion. Saying, "When your mind takes a leap, follow it," my father invited me to step into the poem with him. As we wandered through, I described where I was, what I saw, and things I felt. When we emerged, I knew that words could create noise and pictures and that I was in charge of that poem, of any poem. There is no wrong meaning. My eight-year-old eyes were opened to the power a poem—and I—could wield.

I write poetry each day, turning to Carroll's "Jabberwocky" to remind me what my words should create. I actually recite it daily, in a soft whisper, as I rock my grandson to sleep. I plan to make sure he will know his power, too.

Ithaca

Constantine Cavafy

When you set sail for Ithaca,
wish for the road to be long,
full of adventures, full of knowledge.
The Lestrygonians and the Cyclopes,
an angry Poseidon—do not fear.
You will never find such on your path,
if your thoughts remain lofty, and your spirit
and body are touched by a fine emotion.
The Lestrygonians and the Cyclopes,
a savage Poseidon you will not encounter,
if you do not carry them within your spirit,
if your spirit does not place them before you.
Wish for the road to be long.
Many the summer mornings to be when
with what pleasure, what joy
you will enter ports seen for the first time.
Stop at Phoenician markets,
and purchase the fine goods,
nacre and coral, amber and ebony,
and exquisite perfumes of all sorts,
the most delicate fragances you can find.
To many Egyptian cities you must go,
to learn and learn from the cultivated.
Always keep Ithaca in your mind.
To arrive there is your final destination.
But do not hurry the voyage at all.
It is better for it to last many years,
and when old to rest in the island,
rich with all you have gained on the way,
not expecting Ithaca to offer you wealth.
Ithaca has given you the beautiful journey.
Without her you would not have set out on the road.

Nothing more does she have to give you.
And if you find her poor, Ithaca has not deceived you.
Wise as you have become, with so much experience,
you must already have understood what Ithacas mean.

Alexander G. Zestos, of Charlottesville, writes:

During my 2003 Valedictory address at the York High School commencement, I quoted from Constantine Cavafy's "Ithaka" (translated here as "Ithaca"). The poem offered a fitting allegory for my journey from high school to college, from adolescence to manhood. Cavafy's vivid metaphors rang true then, and they ring as true today as they did when he penned them.

We often overlook life's journey through our many struggles and only see an end goal. After the Greek victory of the Trojan War, Odysseus labored tirelessly on his journey towards Ithaka and his beloved Penelope. He encountered the cyclops, lotus eaters, sirens, Circe, and Kalypso in his seemingly never-ending trek towards home. Cavafy warns that Ithaka is the ultimate destination, but one should not be alarmed "if you find her poor."

Many times we yearn for something so long and so greatly that we are disappointed when we finally receive it. However, what Ithaka gives you, ultimately, is the trip you embark on from the beginning. It provides the desire and motivation for your eventual voyage.

As I have continued my life's Odyssey, I have sought Ithaka in myriad goals, such as gaining admission to a prestigious university, pursuing a career, and starting a family. During my many highs and lows, I have always appreciated the journey that has molded my life thus far and the many twists and turns in my path. Though that journey is still in its early stages, I always have Ithaka in sight, while enjoying the ride along the way.

In the Desert

Stephen Crane

In the desert
I saw a creature, naked, bestial,
Who, squatting upon the ground,
Held his heart in his hands,
And ate of it.
I said, "Is it good, friend?"
"It is bitter—bitter," he answered;

"But I like it
"Because it is bitter,
"And because it is my heart."

Chad Carter, of Fredericksburg, writes:

I was a teenager by the 1980s, a boy of shy, fearful demeanor. I had emerged from a separated home into a paranoid one; my mother's increasing mental illness, which had driven away my father, burrowed an identity beneath her frenzied cheeks and frizzled hair. I grew more isolated, withdrawn within high school's caste, a poverty-line kid who wore the same pair of oversized pants for a week at a time. All of my childhood monsters—the ones in the dark, the ones outside my window at night, the ones deep in the tool shed—they attended school with me, confident as torturers in stone-washed Gap jeans.

When the time came to find an identity for myself, an English teacher noted my turn of phrase and proclaimed I was a "writer." In a how-to book on creative writing, which read like a manual for repairing a leaky faucet, I encountered Crane's "In the Desert." The poem was a hallucination in which I saw myself exposed ("naked"), bestial ("poor"), and a creature ("removed"). And I had long recognized I wanted nothing more than to gorge on this new identity, this "writer." My purpose was made clear: I would forever devour only this tough, marbled muscle. And for twenty-eight years, I have done nothing but.

I felt a Funeral, in my Brain

Emily Dickinson

I felt a Funeral, in my Brain,
And Mourners to and fro
Kept treading – treading – till it seemed
That Sense was breaking through—

And when they all were seated,
A Service, like a Drum –
Kept beating – beating – till I thought
My mind was going numb –

And then I heard them lift a Box
And creak across my Soul
With those same Boots of Lead, again,
Then Space – began to toll,

As all the Heavens were a Bell,
And Being, but an Ear,
And I, and Silence, some strange Race
Wrecked, solitary, here –

And then a Plank in Reason, broke,
And I dropped down, and down –
And hit a World, at every plunge,
And Finished knowing – then –

ॐॐॐ

Thomas Gardner, of Blacksburg, writes:

What I love about this poem is its steely-eyed precision. Dickinson looks back on some sort of mental collapse, but she does so with such a quiet calmness. She uses the funeral as a metaphor to walk us through the event, which happened in her "Brain."

There were several stages, she says. First, she seemed to be just on the edge of making "Sense" of some sort of problem. She compares that to "Mourners" at a funeral, walking back and forth—exactly the way we feel when we're wrestling and wrestling with something. Then comes a second stage, the mind not able to make any more progress with the problem beating against it and "going numb." A remarkable moment occurs in the third and fourth stanzas, and the heavy boots of the pallbearers and the church's bell help us picture it—the mind, unable to process the world, simply took it all in, like an "Ear" being filled with the tolling bell of "all the Heavens." She felt shipwrecked, abandoned, washed up in a world with "Silence" her only companion. After that, the ending seems inevitable: a "Plank" in reason broke, and she tumbled "down, and down." How fascinating though that, without reason, there were still "World[s]" to be glimpsed as she fell. And how fascinating, too, that when she had "Finished" the work of knowing, she hadn't finished the work of living.

Dickinson implies that she discovered there a deep, receptive openness to the world. She has returned to the world of reason now, but she writes out of the other sort of knowledge. How good it is to know this.

The Show is not the Show

Emily Dickinson

The Show is not the Show
But they that go –
Menagerie to me
My neighbor be –
Fair Play –
Both went to see –

Timothy "Tim" Kaine, of Richmond, writes:

There are different poems that assume importance in the passing seasons of life.

I have a small study at home with windows on three sides. I can watch nature unfold — flowers and trees, birds, rabbits and squirrels, people walking their dogs — every day throughout the year. I keep binoculars close and also a copy of Emily Dickinson's COLLECTED POEMS because they are so filled with wonder at the natural world. "The Show is not the Show" is one I fixed on recently after not paying much attention to it in earlier treks through the book.

I love this simple poem for many reasons. Being deeply involved in politics is a bit like being in a show, with the lights bright (and even harsh) at center stage. But the poem reminds us that the real show is offstage, in the lives of spectators, or voters, or early morning passersby. It's a humbling thought — and a wise one.

Death Be Not Proud

John Donne

Death, be not proud, though some have called thee
Mighty and dreadful, for thou art not so;
For those whom thou think'st thou do dost overthrow
Die not, poor Death, nor yet canst thou kill me.
From rest and sleep, which but thy pictures be,
Much pleasure; then from thee much more must flow,
And soonest our best men with thee do go,
Rest of their bones, and soul's delivery.
Thou art slave to fate, chance, kings, and desperate men,
And dost with poison, war, and sickness dwell,
And poppy or charms can make us sleep as well
And better than thy stroke; why swell'st thou then?
One short sleep past, we wake eternally,
And death shall be no more; Death thou shalt die.

Lauvonda Lynn M. Young, of Palmyra, writes:

I became acquainted with John Donne's "Death Be Not Proud" in September 1955, when my brother, Jack Nelson, five years of age, died after a gunshot ripped open his chest. Jackie and our brother, Paul Edward, were playing cowboys and indians. Paul decided it would be fun to use an uncle's rifle—one allegedly unloaded and secured in a locked storage shed. A single bullet produced a quick death. I was ten years old, too young to care about poetry, but old enough to be cumbered with sadness.

Prior to the founding of funeral chapels, viewings took place in homes. I was standing beside my brother's casket in our cramped parlor when I first heard someone read Donne's poem.

Over the years, I returned to "Death Be Not Proud" by placing copies in sympathy cards and including the verses in funeral announcements. In college creative writing classes, Donne's poem was discussed often. It was easy for me to agree with others that Donne declares death does not kill the soul: "Die not, poor death, nor yet canst thou kill me" and "One short sleep past, we wake eternally."

I stay conflicted, though, because I'm not religious; but I am spiritual, and Donne's poem gives me hope there is an afterlife. I derive solace envisioning my brother, whole again, waiting to embrace me upon arrival. Still five years old in my vision, Jackie has the wisdom of the wisest.

To the Virginian Voyage

Michael Drayton

You brave Heroique Minds,
Worthy your countries name,
  That honour still pursue,
  Goe, and subdue,
Whilst loyt'ring Hinds
Lurke here at home, with shame.

Britans, you stay too long,
Quickly aboord bestow you,
  And with a merry Gale
  Swell your stretch'd Sayle,
With Vowes as strong,
As the Winds that blow you.

Your Course securely steere,
West and by South forth keepe,
  Rocks, Lee-shores, nor Sholes,
  When *Eolus* scowles,
You need not feare,
So absolute the Deepe.

And cheerfully at Sea,
Successe you still intice,
  To get the Pearle and Gold,
  And ours to hold,
Virginia,
Earth's onely Paradise.

Where nature hath in store
Fowle, Venison, and Fish,
  And the fruitfull'st Soyle,
  Without your Toyle,

Three Harvests more,
All greater than your wish.

And the ambitious Vine
Crownes with his purple Masse,
  The Cedar reaching hie
  To kisse the Sky,
The Cypresse, Pine
And use-full Sassafras.

To whose, the golden Age
Still Natures lawes doth give,
  No other Cares that tend,
  But Them to defend
From Winters age,
That long there doth not live.

When as the Lushious smell
Of that delicious Land,
  Above the Seas that flowes,
  The cleere Wind throwes,
Your Hearts to swell
Approching the deare Strand.

In kenning of the Shore,
(Thanks to God first given,)
  O you, the happy'st men,
  Be Frolike then,
Let Cannons roare,
Frighting the wide Heaven.

And in Regions farre
Such *Heroes* bring yee foorth,
  As those from whom We came,
  And plant Our name,
Under that Starre
Not knowne unto our North.

And as there Plenty growes
Of Lawrell every where,
  Apollo's Sacred tree,
  You it may see,
A Poets Browes
To crowne, that may sing there.

Thy Voyage attend,
Industrious
  Whose Reading shall inflame
  Men to seeke Fame,
And much commend
To after-times thy Wit.

❧❧❧

Laura L. Close, of Fairfax, writes:

For reasons which are too many to name, "To the Virginian Voyage" is a poem which has not only my name written on it, but also the names of many others: all who believe in adventure, the ocean, the Promised Land, and the preservation of such natural resources as the cypress, the cedar, and the sassafras!

In today's mixed-up world of travel and search for a place of belonging, this poem gives me an area of centeredness and quietness from which to draw hope and inspiration. It is a reminder to me of the many places men and women have walked for centuries, the many roads they (and we) have taken and continue to take, crossing great distances to see what we might see, for that is perhaps what we must all do.

Whenever I read this poem by Michael Drayton, I am filled with gratitude that I was born in this state and am able to call it home. I have left Virginia many times, but I have returned to it as many, even though a little bit of my blood, like the blood of those early voyagers, came from "Great Britannia" and did not hail from these shores.

Self-Reliance

Ralph Waldo Emerson

Henceforth, please God, forever I forego
The yoke of men's opinions. I will be
Light-hearted as a bird, and live with God.
I find him in the bottom of my heart,
I hear continually his voice therein.

* * *

The little needle always knows the North,
The little bird remembereth his note,
And this wise Seer within me never errs.
I never taught it what it teaches me;
I only follow, when I act aright.

* * *

And when I am entombed in my place,
Be it remembered of a single man,
He never, though he dearly loved his race,
For fear of human eyes swerved from his plan.

Oh what is Heaven but the fellowship
Of minds that each can stand against the world
By its own meek and incorruptible will?

The days pass over me
And I am still the same;
The aroma of my life is gone
With the flower with which it came.

෧෧෧

William "Bill" Bolling, of Richmond, writes:

I grew up in a small coal-mining town in southern West Virginia. My parents didn't have much, but at an early age they instilled in me certain values that have remained with me all my life. My father was in many ways a hard man, but also loving and kind. He was very self-reliant, and one of the things he taught me was to be self-sufficient. My dad believed in working hard and depending on no one but himself and his own good judgment. That had been his experience in life.

One of the first poems I remember learning when I got to school was "If" by the British writer Rudyard Kipling. It seemed to sum up a lot of the lessons my parents had taught me. Since then, I have learned that there are other things that are also important in life, and that you can't always rely only on yourself. You have to rely on your faith, as expressed by the American thinker and poet, Ralph Waldo Emerson, in the poem selected here, "Self-Reliance." In addition, I have learned that you need your family and good friends to help you along the way. And so both Kipling's and Emerson's poems, with the thoughts they embrace about self-reliance and having the proper values, have remained favorite poems of mine throughout the years.

Advice to Myself

Louise Erdrich

Leave the dishes.
Let the celery rot in the bottom drawer of the refrigerator
and an earthen scum harden on the kitchen floor.
Leave the black crumbs in the bottom of the toaster.
Throw the cracked bowl out and don't patch the cup.
Don't patch anything. Don't mend. Buy safety pins.
Don't even sew on a button.
Let the wind have its way, then the earth
that invades as dust and then the dead
foaming up in gray rolls underneath the couch.
Talk to them. Tell them they are welcome.
Don't keep all the pieces of the puzzles
or the doll's tiny shoes in pairs, don't worry
who uses whose toothbrush or if anything
matches, at all.
Except one word to another. Or a thought.
Pursue the authentic—decide first
what is authentic,
then go after it with all your heart.
Your heart, that place
you don't even think of cleaning out.
That closet stuffed with savage mementos.
Don't sort the paper clips from screws from saved baby teeth
or worry if we're all eating cereal for dinner
again. Don't answer the telephone, ever,
or weep over anything at all that breaks.
Pink molds will grow within those sealed cartons
in the refrigerator. Accept new forms of life
and talk to the dead
who drift in through the screened windows, who collect
patiently on the tops of food jars and books.

Recycle the mail, don't read it, don't read anything
except what destroys
the insulation between yourself and your experience
or what pulls down or what strikes at or what shatters
this ruse you call necessity.

࿐࿐࿐

Guy Terrell, of North Chesterfield, writes:

I lost my last full-time job in 2007. I was fifty-seven years old and unaware that finding another full-time job at my age was unlikely. Not knowing the outcome of things was the greatest gift I could have received; otherwise I might have given up when the odds turned against me.

For the last six years, I have worked as a contractor where my labor is paid for by the hour with no benefits, no paid holidays, no vacation, no external incentives. All the time, I've felt I was worth more to the world (and to myself!) than what my job situation implied, but I could not see how.

I came across Louise Erdrich's poem "Advice to Myself" in 2012. I have always written in stolen moments and finished nothing. ("No one remembers what you started," I read somewhere.) I wanted to see what I could achieve, but the admonition to stay at my job for as long as I was able to drove me. What right did I or do any of us have to our dreams?

Reading this poem was like reaching the last chapter in a very long book. I'd spent my whole life afraid to take the ultimate personal risk: to write. There was no other way to describe it. This poem became my personal Emancipation Proclamation. I would at last take possession of my own heart, my own dreams. I would employ myself; I would become a writer full time!

The Road Not Taken

Robert Frost

Two roads diverged in a yellow wood,
And sorry I could not travel both
And be one traveler, long I stood
And looked down one as far as I could
To where it bent in the undergrowth;

Then took the other, as just as fair,
And having perhaps the better claim,
Because it was grassy and wanted wear;
Though as for that the passing there
Had worn them really about the same,

And both that morning equally lay
In leaves no step had trodden black.
Oh, I kept the first for another day!
Yet knowing how way leads on to way,
I doubted if I should ever come back.

I shall be telling this with a sigh
Somewhere ages and ages hence:
Two roads diverged in a wood, and I—
I took the one less traveled by,
And that has made all the difference.

৵৵৵

Keyada M. Richardson, of Hampton, writes:

As an English teacher and genuine lover of all things poetic, I have come across many poems that have impacted me greatly, but Robert Frost's poem "The Road Not Taken" has unrelentingly been nearest to me. I find that this poem speaks to my inner self because as time progresses, I seem to be called to make more and more difficult decisions.

I consider myself to be quite indecisive and sometimes find it close to impossible to make a quick decision, because of the fear of making the wrong choice. It seems that at the precipice of reaching a new accomplishment or chapter in my life, I am always forced to make a hard decision about the next chapter, and I find myself, like the traveler in this poem, contemplating which path would be the most beneficial.

I know full well that making a concrete decision means journeying along a path that will leave me to wonder what would have come from choosing the other path. There's always the possibility of regret, as expressed in the poem; however, the poem is personally near to me, because it actually helps me to live without regret over my decisions. Like the poem's traveler, I find myself concluding that it's best not to wonder "what if" or "what could've been." I always tell myself that I made the right decision for me—and so far, to my satisfaction, that belief "has made all the difference."

We Are Virginia Tech

Nikki Giovanni

We are Virginia Tech.

We are sad today, and we will be sad for quite a while. We are not moving on, we are embracing our mourning.

We are Virginia Tech.

We are strong enough to stand tall tearlessly, we are brave enough to bend to cry, and we are sad enough to know that we must laugh again.

We are Virginia Tech.

We do not understand this tragedy. We know we did nothing to deserve it, but neither does a child in Africa dying of AIDS, neither do the invisible children walking the night away to avoid being captured by the rogue army, neither does the baby elephant watching his community being devastated for ivory, neither does the Mexican child looking for fresh water, neither does the Appalachian infant killed in the middle of the night in his crib in the home his father built with his own hands being run over by a boulder because the land was destabilized. No one deserves a tragedy.

We are Virginia Tech.

The Hokie Nation embraces our own and reaches out with open heart and hands to those who offer their hearts and minds. We are strong, and brave, and innocent, and unafraid.

We are better than we think and not quite what we want to be. We are alive to the imaginations and the possibilities. We will continue to invent the future through our blood and tears and through all our sadness.

We are the Hokies.

We will prevail.

We will prevail.

We will prevail.

We are Virginia Tech.

John Graves Warner, of Virginia Beach, writes:

Poets have a way of helping make sense of the senseless. It was while working on the public television series Virginia Currents that I came into contact with the Virginia Tech tragedy in which thirty-three people perished. My producing partner May-Lily Lee and I created a special broadcast, turning to poets Gregory Donovan of Virginia Commonwealth University and Nikki Giovanni of Virginia Tech. In our studios, Greg quoted Emerson:

"The life of man is a self-evolving circle, which, from a ring imperceptibly small, rushes on all sides outwards to new and larger circles, and that without end. The extent to which this generation of circles, wheel without wheel, will go, depends on the force or truth of the individual soul."

What Greg shared was meaningful, and we're pretty certain there were no other local broadcasts that week turning to poets for insight. That same week, at a memorial convocation, Nikki Giovanni read "We Are Virginia Tech." It was almost like a call to arms, in a revolutionary way, in the style of spoken word. It was important that she was there that day, and her reading truly helped with the emotions of the moment. She definitely had an impact on the community with this piece, which still rings true today.

Remember

Joy Harjo

Remember the sky that you were born under,
know each of the star's stories.
Remember the moon, know who she is. I met her
in a bar once in Iowa City.
Remember the sun's birth at dawn, that is the
strongest point of time. Remember sundown
and the giving away to night.
Remember your birth, how your mother struggled
to give you form and breath. You are evidence of
her life, and her mother's, and hers.
Remember your father. He is your life also.
Remember the earth whose skin you are:
red earth, black earth, yellow earth, white earth
brown earth, we are earth.
Remember the plants, trees, animal life who all have their
tribes, their families, their histories, too. Talk to them,
listen to them. They are alive poems.
Remember the wind. Remember her voice. She knows the
origin of this universe. I heard her singing Kiowa war
dance songs at the corner of Fourth and Central once.
Remember that you are all people and that all people are you.
Remember that you are this universe and that this universe is you.
Remember that all is in motion, is growing, is you.
Remember that language comes from this.
Remember the dance that language is, that life is.
Remember.

ॐॐॐ

Donna Price Henry, of Wise, writes:

As Chancellor of the University of Virginia's College at Wise, it is important for me to demonstrate my values through my actions. Strong beliefs developed in my life history — "the sky that [I was] born under" — support sound leadership and decision making.

My nearest poem, Joy Harjo's "Remember," reflects my belief that a quality liberal arts education provides students with diverse perspectives from which to view the world. As Harjo says: "you are all people and…all people are you." Diversity of knowledge encourages greater connectedness within our communities. The creation of a civil and sustainable society is dependent on this knowledge and engagement.

I am often asked to describe my vision for the College. I respond that my vision includes the collective voice of the College community. Again, I hear Harjo urging: "you are this universe and… this universe is you." Our vision is rooted in the strengths of all those who live the mission of the College in their classes and offices every day.

Communication among us is essential to ensure that the community understands the interconnectedness between whom we say we are and what we do. Here, too, I hear Harjo's admonition: "Remember the dance that language is, that life is." Clear communication of our mission attracts students who choose to come to us for their education. They learn that the College experience is more than learning about a discipline. It includes learning to collaborate, connecting knowledge to issues in society. As the poem insists: "all is in motion, is growing, is you." The students embody the mission with their service projects, academic achievements, and engagement of the community.

To achieve the vision of the College, it is important for me to remember, with the kind of embrace that this poem expresses, that my leadership is grounded in the broader community that I serve.

Casabianca

Felicia Dorothea Hemans

The boy stood on the burning deck
Whence all but him had fled;
The flame that lit the battle's wreck
Shone round him o'er the dead.

Yet beautiful and bright he stood,
As born to rule the storm;
A creature of heroic blood,
A proud, though childlike form.

The flames rolled on – he would not go
Without his father's word;
That father, faint in death below,
His voice no longer heard.

He called aloud – "Say, father, say,
If yet my task is done?"
He knew not that the chieftain lay
Unconscious of his son.

"Speak, father!" once again he cried,
"If I may yet be gone!"
And but the booming shots replied,
And fast the flames rolled on.

Upon his brow he felt their breath,
And in his waving hair,
And looked from that lone post of death
In still, yet brave despair.

And shouted but once more aloud,
"My father! must I stay?"
While o'er him fast, through sail and shroud,
The wreathing fires made way.

They wrapt the ship in splendor wild,
They caught the flag on high,
And streamed above the gallant child,
Like banners in the sky.

There came a burst of thunder sound –
The boy – oh! where was he?
Ask of the winds that far around
With fragments strewed the sea! –

With mast, and helm, and pennon fair
That well had borne their part –
But the noblest thing that perished there
Was that young, faithful heart.

Richard C. Nottingham, of Free Union, writes:

I remember one evening my father brought home the coffee-table book PARLOR POETRY. I asked him what "parlor poetry" was. He informed me that before the advent of radio and television, people would read poems in their living rooms for entertainment.

I started reading. All the poems had stories, but I was only eight or nine years old at that time, and not many of them interested me. And then I got to "Casabianca." I read the poem once, twice…. Afterwards, I would lie in bed at night and picture the battle. I would place myself as the boy. I was just as brave and courageous as he was.

As I've grown older, I look at things differently. I try to find the spiritual principle that underlies every human event. I can still picture myself as the little boy on the deck, but today I look for sustaining values. The boy's bravery stands out, his unbelievable courage. There are others as well. The unconditional love he had for his father. The respect. The patience it took, and the perseverance, as he waited for an answer. These are lessons I learn from the poem even today.

Every time I read "Casabianca," I thank my father for bringing home the book that started my interest in poetry.

As I Grew Older

Langston Hughes

It was a long time ago.
I have almost forgotten my dream.
But it was there then,
In front of me,
Bright like a sun—
My dream.
And then the wall rose,
Rose slowly,
Slowly,
Between me and my dream.
Rose until it touched the sky—
The wall.
Shadow.
I am black.
I lie down in the shadow.
No longer the light of my dream before me,
Above me.
Only the thick wall.
Only the shadow.
My hands!
My dark hands!
Break through the wall!
Find my dream!
Help me to shatter this darkness,
To smash this night,
To break this shadow
Into a thousand lights of sun,
Into a thousand whirling dreams
Of sun!

ക്ക്ക

Erick Green, of Winchester, writes:

I grew up loving the game of basketball. It was what I wanted to do with my life. My dreams of becoming a professional basketball player seemed easy at the time. I was naïve, and like any other kid I figured it would be easy.

"As I Grew Older" is about achieving goals. Langston Hughes explains that although there were obstacles, he had to persist in order to arrive at his dream. The relation I have with the poem is a relation with the man behind the words. I feel his pain, his desire. Finding obstacles in the way of one's dreams is one of life's most painful realizations. It means moving one step forward and three steps back.

My freshman year at Virginia Tech as a basketball player wasn't what I expected it to be. I would receive hurtful emails telling me that I was a waste of a scholarship. I had to watch my peers on the team play, one step closer to their dreams, while I sat on the bench. I struggled with confidence, but in my struggle I found hope. That year I decided to shatter not only the negativity in my mind, but also the negativity around me, in order to reach "the light of my dream."

I have not yet reached my dream of becoming a professional basketball player, but every day I'm one step closer to it. "As I Grew Older" inspires me not to let obstacles change my future. Langston Hughes's dream was that of African-Americans overcoming racial discrimination. For me, it's that of becoming a professional basketball player and meeting life's challenges, on and off the court.

When I'm surrounded by anxiety, doubt, and hardship, my dreams will be like hands that "break through the wall" toward the "sun," creating new rays of hope, ambition, and purpose.

Abou Ben Adhem

James Henry Leigh Hunt

Abou Ben Adhem (may his tribe increase!)
Awoke one night from a deep dream of peace,
And saw, within the moonlight in his room,
Making it rich and like a lily in bloom,
An angel writing in a book of gold:—
Exceeding peace had made Ben Adhem bold,
And to the presence in the room he said,
"What writest thou?"—The vision raised its head,
And with a look made of all sweet accord,
Answered, "The names of those who love the Lord."
"And is mine one?" said Abou. "Nay, not so,"
Replied the angel. Abou spoke more low,
But cheerly still; and said, "I pray thee, then,
Write me as one that loved his fellow men."

　　The angel wrote and vanished. The next night
It came again, with a great wakening light,
And showed the names whom love of God had blessed,
And, lo! Ben Adhem's name led all the rest!

Adele Richards Oberhelman, of Williamsburg, writes:

My mother was not much of a churchgoer but she kept a King James Bible on the coffee table. I can't remember ever seeing her read it, so I suspect she simply perceived it as a symbol of reverence and a kind of talisman. She might have felt it was a testament to her piety.

I do remember, though, as through a haze, that a copy of the poem "Abou Ben Adhem" appeared from time to time; I can't remember where or why. I also know that a copy was found among her personal papers.

My mother never turned away a hungry person. More than one fried-egg sandwich was eaten by someone out of work on our back steps, and she always collected for the March of Dimes. She loved children—all children. We were taught never to make fun of the disabled or odd-looking and always to be kind.

Although not formally religious myself, I have found meaning in the words of the poem, and I suspect she set much store by them as well.

Hardy Bird

for Felix Stefanile

A. M. Juster

When I can hear my raucous sparrows sing,
I shed some gravity, then brace to fly
until their urgent chords start softening.

We echo notes like these to justify
dark hours with blank pages—time we spend
in ways no predator can comprehend.
Like sparrows pulling grubs from rotting oaks,
we peck obsessively; and if we pry
some morsels from the wood that satisfy
demands for sustenance, we try to coax
our throats to warble songs no soul has heard.

We are indebted to the steadfast man
who hears the sorrow of the striving bird
and spreads whatever crumbs of bread he can.

Patricia Policarpio Martin, of Falls Church, writes:

A.M. Juster's poem "Hardy Bird" touches me personally. Phrases like "pry/ some morsels" and "coax/ our throats" express a desire to go beyond the surface, to be original, and to attach meaning to what we do. They also seem to express a struggle to be conscientious and productive at work. Since I am a research analyst for the government and write for a living, the poem exhorts me to dig deeply and to uncover truth and its implications: "warble songs no soul has heard." In contrast to Richard Wilbur's celebratory "Mayflies," another gem I enjoy reading, Juster's "Hardy Bird" involves doing.

The poem is meaningful to me because it emphasizes the need to be creatively inspired and motivated in what we do, a duality that leads to balancing work and reward. At the end, Juster appreciates the dependable sources who help the "sparrows" survive. I think of mentors, teachers, colleagues, and friends…. Sparrows taking flight or singing signify both inspiration and accomplishment. I can't fly; actually I can't even sing as I'd like to, but my work and my passions do take flight, and I can fly with them. However, this will occur only if, like the sparrows, I "peck obsessively" and appreciate the "crumbs" from the "steadfast man."

It is little known that A.M. Juster is the pseudonym for former Social Security Commissioner Michael Astrue, and such dual roles as poet and public servant are exceedingly rare. Imagine a federal bureaucrat by day and a poet by night. To be able to pull off this dual feat is inspiring to me. This creative thinker may have uncovered not only a successful creative outlet but also a new work/life model, an antidote to work-related trials.

If

Rudyard Kipling

If you can keep your head when all about you
    Are losing theirs and blaming it on you,
If you can trust yourself when all men doubt you,
    But make allowance for their doubting too;
If you can wait and not be tired by waiting,
    Or being lied about, don't deal in lies,
Or being hated, don't give way to hating,
    And yet don't look too good, nor talk too wise:

If you can dream—and not make dreams your master;
    If you can think—and not make thoughts your aim;
If you can meet with Triumph and Disaster
    And treat those two impostors just the same;
If you can bear to hear the truth you've spoken
    Twisted by knaves to make a trap for fools,
Or watch the things you gave your life to, broken,
    And stoop and build 'em up with worn-out tools:

If you can make one heap of all your winnings
    And risk it on one turn of pitch-and-toss,
And lose, and start again at your beginnings
    And never breathe a word about your loss;
If you can force your heart and nerve and sinew
    To serve your turn long after they are gone,
And so hold on when there is nothing in you
    Except the Will which says to them: 'Hold on!'

If you can talk with crowds and keep your virtue,
    Or walk with Kings—nor lose the common touch,

If neither foes nor loving friends can hurt you,
    If all men count with you, but none too much;
If you can fill the unforgiving minute
    With sixty seconds' worth of distance run,
Yours is the Earth and everything that's in it,
    And—which is more—you'll be a Man, my son!

ৡৡৡ

Carroll W. Dale, of Wise, writes:

I have selected "If" by Rudyard Kipling, with special attention to the first two lines, which relate most to me. They are a recipe for living, a guide for all humanity to live by.

As a young man striving to find my way in the world, I often sought words of wisdom and knowledge from others to help me be successful and to be a better man. Kipling's words really personify what one needs to hear when self-doubt and anguish come to a man in the middle of the night. It is important to keep yourself focused and to remember that we are masters of our own destination. That there is a bigger Power and a bigger purpose. I believe if a person could abide by the lines in this poem, that person would be close to sainthood.

Aubade

Philip Larkin

I work all day, and get half-drunk at night.
Waking at four to soundless dark, I stare.
In time the curtain-edges will grow light.
Till then I see what's always really there:
Unresting death, a whole day nearer now,
Making all thought impossible but how
And where and when I shall myself die.
Arid interrogation: but the dread
Of dying, and being dead,
Flashes afresh to hold and horrify.

The mind blanks at the glare. Not in remorse
—The good not done, the love not given, time
Torn off unused—nor wretchedly because
An only life can take so long to climb
Clear of its wrong beginnings, and may never;
But at the total emptiness for ever,
The sure extinction that we travel to
And shall be lost in always. Not to be here,
Not to be anywhere,
And soon; nothing more terrible, nothing more true.

This is a special way of being afraid
No trick dispels. Religion used to try,
That vast moth-eaten musical brocade
Created to pretend we never die,
And specious stuff that says *No rational being*
Can fear a thing it will not feel, not seeing
That this is what we fear—no sight, no sound,
No touch or taste or smell, nothing to think with,
Nothing to love or link with,
The anaesthetic from which none come round.

And so it stays just on the edge of vision,
A small unfocused blur, a standing chill

That slows each impulse down to indecision.
Most things may never happen: this one will,
And realization of it rages out
In furnace-fear when we are caught without
People or drink. Courage is no good:
It means not scaring others. Being brave
Lets no one off the grave.
Death is no different whined at than withstood.

Slowly light strengthens, and the room takes shape.
It stands plain as a wardrobe, what we know,
Have always known, know that we can't escape,
Yet can't accept. One side will have to go.
Meanwhile telephones crouch, getting ready to ring
In locked-up offices, and all the uncaring
Intricate rented world begins to rouse.
The sky is white as clay, with no sun.
Work has to be done.
Postmen like doctors go from house to house.

❧ ❧ ❧

Andrew Cain, of Richmond, writes:

What an undertaking it is to sift one's history for not a favorite poem so much as a nearest poem and then to present it honestly as it was and is, with an intimacy that does not permit critical discipline or clinical distance. The usual tools won't do, nor will the body of poetry immured in memory. This labor requires daring the personal and the attendant risks of embarrassment. So, I waited to write this. Time stretched on until I was by change of residence required to manhandle my poetry collection. Of course the book appeared and with it the poem. Philip Larkin's "Aubade" seemed at two and twenty written to me as I was, and has, now exhumed, undiminished power.

The power of "Aubade" lies in its simplicity. Larkin here is neither vague nor lyrical, and the straight-forward way the poem fits line and sense, sense and sentence into a single unit with a line like the breathtaking, "Death is no different whined at than withstood" compels.

The poem's opening, "I work all day, and get half-drunk at night," has the workman's set and drive, the fighter's jab and cross. It reached across that formidable distance that working stiffs maintain against anything academic and pretentious and hauled me up by the collar bones. From that line to the penultimate, "Work has to be done," is nothing slack or lyrical. Even the telephone's crouch is a muscular prelude to its pounce, and then, the simile's cat and mouse. How are postmen like doctors? It is as fine a question as ever. Something to consider while climbing clear of wrong beginnings.

Christmas Bells

Henry Wadsworth Longfellow

I heard the bells on Christmas Day
Their old, familiar carols play,
   And wild and sweet
   The words repeat
Of peace on earth, good-will to men!

And thought how, as the day had come,
The belfries of all Christendom
   Had rolled along
   The unbroken song
Of peace on earth, good-will to men!

Till ringing, singing on its way,
The world revolved from night to day,
   A voice, a chime,
   A chant sublime
Of peace on earth, good-will to men!

Then from each black, accursed mouth
The cannon thundered in the South,
   And with the sound
   The carols drowned
Of peace on earth, good-will to men!

It was as if an earthquake rent
The hearth-stones of a continent,
   And made forlorn
   The households born
Of peace on earth, good-will to men!

And in despair I bowed my head;
"There is no peace on earth," I said;

"For hate is strong,
  And mocks the song
Of peace on earth, good-will to men!"

Then pealed the bells more loud and deep:
"God is not dead, nor doth He sleep;
  The Wrong shall fail,
  The Right prevail,
With peace on earth, good-will to men."

❦❦❦

H. Morgan Griffith, of Salem, writes:

As a father to three young children, I was heartbroken upon hearing of the heinous, criminal act that took place in Newtown, Connecticut, in December 2012. No words could describe the senseless crime that took the lives of so many children. Any tragedy is difficult to understand, but especially difficult to comprehend are those that impact young people. We, in western Virginia, know all too well that senseless violence like this has no place in our society. Just a year before, I had written about American poet Henry Wadsworth Longfellow and his poem "Christmas Bells;" the poem and song became especially poignant to me after this tragedy.

Having suffered through years of great despair following the tragic loss of his wife and the injury of his son Charles in the War Between the States, Longfellow wrote "Christmas Bells," which became the basis for the carol "I Heard the Bells on Christmas Day." The poem tells of its narrator's despair that "hate is strong/ And mocks the song/ Of peace on earth, good-will to men"—until he hears the ringing of the bells, which celebrate the power of faith and offer great hope.

Just like Longfellow, we have witnessed despair and evil, and sadly, we witness these things again and again. But "God is not dead; nor doth He sleep." Even as we mourn and yes, cry, we celebrate the Christmas season every year, as we remember these words from the Gospel of John: "God so loved the world that He gave His only begotten Son, that whosoever believeth in Him should not perish, but have everlasting life."

A Psalm of Life

What The Heart Of The Young Man Said To The Psalmist

Henry Wadsworth Longfellow

Tell me not in mournful numbers,
　　Life is but an empty dream!
For the soul is dead that slumbers,
　　And things are not what they seem.

Life is real! Life is earnest!
　　And the grave is not its goal;
Dust thou art, to dust returnest,
　　Was not spoken of the soul.

Not enjoyment, and not sorrow,
　　Is our destined end or way;
But to act, that each to-morrow
　　Find us farther than to-day.

Art is long, and Time is fleeting,
　　And our hearts, though stout and brave,
Still, like muffled drums, are beating
　　Funeral marches to the grave.

In the world's broad field of battle,
　　In the bivouac of Life,
Be not like dumb, driven cattle!
　　Be a hero in the strife!

Trust no Future, howe'er pleasant!
　　Let the dead Past bury its dead!
Act,—act in the living Present!
　　Heart within, and God o'erhead!

Lives of great men all remind us
    We can make our lives sublime,
And, departing, leave behind us
    Footprints on the sands of time;

Footprints, that perhaps another,
    Sailing o'er life's solemn main,
A forlorn and shipwrecked brother,
    Seeing, shall take heart again.

Let us, then, be up and doing,
    With a heart for any fate;
Still achieving, still pursuing,
    Learn to labor and to wait.

Ronnie Brown, of Richmond, writes:

Over the past three years I have had the privilege of being involved in an incredible program known as Poetry Out Loud: National Recitation Competition. This program encourages our nation's youth to learn about great poetry through memorization and recitation. All students are asked to choose and memorize poems, then recite them in a competition against their peers. I felt that since this was a requirement for the students competing and I'm the State Coordinator, it should be a requirement for me too.

While flipping through POL's printed anthology, the poem that I chose to memorize was "A Psalm of Life: What The Heart Of The Young Man Said To The Psalmist" by Henry Wadsworth Longfellow. Being a young man myself, I soon discovered that the poem resonated with me; it reflected my feelings about life and living.

Most of us are taught that we are born, we go to school, find a "job," have a family, and then we die…. But no! "Tell me not… Life is but an empty dream/… Life is real! Life is earnest!/ And the grave is not its goal." We are told to fit in, to keep our heads down. No! "Be not like dumb driven cattle!/ Be a hero in the strife!" And again, we are cautioned that the life we're given is the life with which we're stuck. No! "Lives of great men all remind us/ We can make our lives sublime…."

This is my nearest poem because it is who I am; it is how I live every day of my life.

The Arrow and the Song

Henry Wadsworth Longfellow

I shot an arrow into the air,
It fell to earth, I knew not where;
For, so swiftly it flew, the sight
Could not follow it in its flight.

I breathed a song into the air,
It fell to earth, I knew not where;
For who has sight so keen and strong,
That it can follow the flight of song?

Long, long afterward, in an oak
I found the arrow, still unbroke;
And the song, from beginning to end,
I found again in the heart of a friend.

June Forte, of Woodbridge, writes:

My first encounter with Henry Wadsworth Longfellow occurred when I was in grammar school. In the middle of a history lesson, my normally soft-spoken fourth-grade teacher suddenly declared in a rich and melodic voice, "Listen, my children, and you shall hear of the midnight ride of Paul Revere." What better tool to engrain the valiant start of the American Revolution in an impressionable schoolgirl's memory than a recitation of Longfellow's "The Midnight Ride of Paul Revere."

But it was in English class that I found a lifelong connection with his "The Arrow and the Song." This poem has a variety of interpretations, but the reality of poetry is that it offers a slightly or sometimes greatly different meaning to each of us. A poem is not complete until there is a reader or listener to interpret it.

For me "The Arrow and the Song" shouts of consequences, in particular the consequences of words spoken that can never be retrieved. We have a choice in every conversation to carelessly send a painful arrow or to mindfully send a joyous song—to a family member, a friend, or a stranger. "The Arrow and the Song" reminds me to reach into the quiver for a song.

Setting the Table

Kindra M. McDonald

When I was young I used to imagine
that Forks were men and Spoons were women.
The Forks would prey on the Spoons
and their sleek, smooth, slightly arched
backs if it weren't for the gallant Knives
on the soft white cotton napkins.

The Knives were long and straight-backed,
gentle and strong, with teeth that warned
The Fork, whose tines rose like claws,
to keep his mouth shut.

My father was both Fork and Knife.
Sometimes he could rise up like the tilted
head of a Fork and with eyes as bright
as silver pierce
me in triplicate.
Other times he was like a Knife, standing tall
warding off enemies, those that break the plates,
and protecting me like a straight-backed soldier,
gently tucking in the white sheets of my bed.

Scooping up soup, I wondered how she could live
with her bent head. Could Spoon learn to meld,
to mold, to change into other forms?
Things not so easily bent, broken and used
to scrape out the dregs that are thrown away.

⊰⊰⊰

Bill Ayres, of Virginia Beach, writes:

This poem reminds me that we think metaphorically all the time. Children are especially good at it; for them, metaphors are what play is all about. It is a very serious thing, for play is how we make sense of the world.

Reading this poem, I see the little girl moving in a circle around the table, setting the silverware in place, making sure things are lined up straight. I hear the pieces clacking against each other, as she tries to do a good job quickly. I imagine her frowning in concentration on her task so she does not hear the voices raised in the other room.

This poem is nearest to me because the metaphor is strong, unusual, and anchored in the every day. I think of it whenever I see a white cloth napkin or I hear someone speak of women being "objectified." It is remarkable how easily we can turn people into things. What is a hero? What is a villain? We use images every day in the way the little girl does so well in the poem—to define, to clarify, to reassure.

Stamping Ground, Bird's Lament

Moondog

Jerry Caldwell, of Roanoke, writes:

In my college days (the late 1970s, most of which were at Brooklyn College), I was exposed to the poetry and music of a blind man who used the name "Moondog." Born Louis Thomas Hardin, he was also known as "The Viking of 6th Avenue" in New York City. His life story is quite amazing, though at the time I had no idea about his background, only that his quick bursts of poetry touched me… made me think and wonder. And they inspired me, as a journalist, to embrace the brevity of the message.

For example, listen to this mini-poem from his recording "Stamping Ground" —

> "Machines were mice and men were lions once upon a time;
> but now that it's the opposite, it's twice upon a time…."

And this one from "Bird's Lament" —

> "The only one who knows this ounce of words is just a token,
> is he who has a tongue to tell that must remain unspoken."

Brief as these two are, they are the poems I have carried in my head and heart for more than three decades.

The Purist

Ogden Nash

I give you now Professor Twist,
A conscientious scientist,
Trustees exclaimed, "He never bungles!"
And sent him off to distant jungles.
Camped on a tropic riverside,
One day he missed his loving bride.
She had, the guide informed him later,
Been eaten by an alligator.
Professor Twist could not but smile.
"You mean," he said, "a crocodile."

Floyd D. Gottwald, Jr., of Richmond, writes:

Two poems that have always commanded my attention are Coleridge's "The Rime of the Ancient Mariner," perhaps because of my interest in the seas and fishing, and Kipling's "Gunga Din," because of my fascination with India as a result of a short service in that country while in the U.S. Army. I would love to take time to memorize both of the above.

One poem that I have memorized and therefore keep very near, and which I have used on several occasions to make a point, is Ogden Nash's "The Purist." There is savvy, even wisdom, in humor, and on every occasion the listener seems to figure out that point.

Kindness

Naomi Shihab Nye

Before you know what kindness really is
you must lose things,
feel the future dissolve in a moment
like salt in a weakened broth.
What you held in your hand,
what you counted and carefully saved,
all this must go so you know
how desolate the landscape can be
between the regions of kindness.
How you ride and ride
thinking the bus will never stop,
the passengers eating maize and chicken
will stare out the window forever.

Before you learn the tender gravity of kindness,
you must travel where the Indian in a white poncho
lies dead by the side of the road.
You must see how this could be you,
how he too was someone
who journeyed through the night with plans
and the simple breath that kept him alive.

Before you show kindness as the deepest thing inside,
you must know sorrow as the other deepest thing.
You must wake up with sorrow.
You must speak to it till your voice
catches the thread of all sorrows
and you see the size of the cloth.

Then it is only kindness that makes sense anymore,
only kindness that ties your shoes

and sends you out into the day to mail letters
                    and purchase bread,
only kindness that raises its head
from the crowd of the world to say
it is I you have been looking for,
and then goes with you everywhere
like a shadow or a friend.

❧ ❧ ❧

Susan Carter Morgan, of Fredericksburg, writes:

Turning sixty changed my life. I am not the first to say this. Age and experience give us perspective about life not possible when we are twenty-five or even thirty-five.

Naomi Shihab Nye writes of kindness, a rather innocuous term for some. What does it mean to be kind, after all? Yet, Nye's poem, which was passed along to me by a friend last year, wrapped its arms around me with its truth. In our ego-driven life, we strive to win, to be right, to get ahead. But at the end of the day, kindness is all that matters. And unfortunately, we don't learn this until we have felt the pain the poet describes.

You must wake up with sorrow.
You must speak to it till your voice
catches the thread of all sorrows
and you see the size of the cloth.

Only then do we learn how to live. And so, I read Nye's words often. When I fail to be kind, the poem brings me back to center, where I try again, keeping it with me "like a shadow or a friend."

War South of the Great Wall

Li Po
Translated by David Hinton

Delirium, battlefields all dark and delirium,
convulsions of men swarm like armies of ants.

A red wheel in thickened air, the sun hangs
above bramble and weed blood's dyed purple,

and crows, their beaks clutching warrior guts,
struggle at flight, grief-glutted, earthbound.

Those on guard atop the Great Wall yesterday
became ghosts in its shadow today. And still,

flags bright everywhere like scattered stars,
the slaughter keeps on. War-drums throbbing:

my husband, my sons—you'll find them all
there, out where war-drums keep throbbing.

James F. Gaines, of Fredericksburg, writes:

This poem resounded with me in several ways. On one level it recalled my mother's family and their tremendous struggles to stay alive, first surviving the persecution of Hitler and the Nazis and then the mindless violence of conflict itself. My father was a professional soldier and met my mother amid that chaos. I longed to follow in his footsteps and earn medals of my own, but the realities of Vietnam dispelled my illusions and turned me into an anti-war activist and sometime self-exile, like Li Po.

Some of the earliest poems I attempted were filled with thundershowers of steel and flame, which rather suddenly had turned, for me, from trappings of epic to instruments of misery and desolation. When I discovered Li Po, I realized that those personal dilemmas which had sprung up in my teenage years were actually millennia-old, echoing in the poetic conscience long before I became aware of them. While I cannot aspire to the level of Master Li Po, I continue to be a pilgrim—or refugee—along a lonely path where he and others trod before.

Richard Cory

Edwin Arlington Robinson

Whenever Richard Cory went down town,
We people on the pavement looked at him:
He was a gentleman from sole to crown,
Clean favored, and imperially slim.

And he was always quietly arrayed,
And he was always human when he talked;
But still he fluttered pulses when he said,
"Good-morning," and he glittered when he walked.

And he was rich—yes, richer than a king—
And admirably schooled in every grace:
In fine, we thought that he was everything
To make us wish that we were in his place.

So on we worked, and waited for the light,
And went without the meat, and cursed the bread;
And Richard Cory, one calm summer night,
Went home and put a bullet through his head.

Maria Perez-Barton, of Herndon, writes:

This poem is nearest to me because I know that looks can be deceiving; my wonderful brother was diagnosed with schizophrenia.

In "Richard Cory" we have a man who is well-to-do and admired, yet he has a secret cross to bear. Mister Cory acts drastically, without warning—and ends his life. With the shootings in Arizona, Colorado, Connecticut, and other places in our country, we need to engage in a dialogue about troubled people and how we might look for warning signs in order to help them. The discourse about gun control is a mere fraction of the issue; mental health concerns must also be brought to the forefront.

I often wonder what would have happened to my brother if my parents had not agreed to look after him for the rest of his life. If he were sent to an institution, would his needs be addressed there? Would he eventually end up in a prison, because of lack of funds for mental health facilities? My brother is not a criminal, and he has not shown any signs of violence, yet there is always the worry about a setback or a negative turn of events. With access to medication, schizophrenia can be controlled. So why are the people who need help not getting it?

Where there's suspicious behavior, that behavior should be addressed. Where there are cries for help, those cries should be answered. It is up to all of us to respond and help one another. The key is to care.

Now I Become Myself

May Sarton

Now I become myself. It's taken
Time, many years and places;
I have been dissolved and shaken,
Worn other people's faces,
Run madly, as if Time were there,
Terribly old, crying a warning,
"Hurry, you will be dead before—"
(What? Before you reach the morning?
Or the end of the poem is clear?
Or love safe in the walled city?)
Now to stand still, to be here,
Feel my own weight and density!
The black shadow on the paper
Is my hand; the shadow of a word
As thought shapes the shaper
Falls heavy on the page, is heard.
All fuses now, falls into place
From wish to action, word to silence,
My work, my love, my time, my face
Gathered into one intense
Gesture of growing like a plant.
As slowly as the ripening fruit
Fertile, detached, and always spent,
Falls but does not exhaust the root,
So all the poem is, can give,
Grows in me to become the song,
Made so and rooted by love.
Now there is time and Time is young.
O, in this single hour I live
All of myself and do not move.
I, the pursued, who madly ran,
Stand still, stand still, and stop the sun!

ॐॐॐ

Nancy Powell, of Hampton, writes:

I found May Sarton's work many years ago when I was stumbling around writing poetry, but not confident enough to say I was a poet. This particular poem, as all of Sarton's work does, speaks to me clearly; it expresses what poetry has done for me: "I, the pursued, who madly ran,/ Stand still, stand still, and stop the sun!"

Sarton had lived in the Northeast where I grew up and where I raised my children, so many of her landscapes are my landscapes, and when she is talking about the seasons — the fall or the winter snows — I know those images and understand her. I almost absorb the work through my skin; it is that visceral for me.

There is another reason why the poem "Now I Become Myself" is the most deeply personal of Sarton's work for me. When I found it, many years ago in upstate New York, I had, in fact, been trying to become myself again after a serious illness. It was a very dark and scary time for me. After years of being merely someone to someone else, I had to be finally me, just me. It was in the midst of all this that I discovered "Now I Become Myself."

The poem would become the guidepost along the road that led me to the place where I could heal, and where I would finally be able to say, "I am a poet; this is who I am." It was a place where, I later discovered, the poems I wrote would not "exhaust the root."

An Innocent in the House of the Dead

Joanna Catherine Scott

You come to me from a nine by seven cell—
one thin-mattressed cot, one high narrow window,
sealed, one obstinate commode.
Your ability to bear is greater than mine
because you have been sorely tested.
What is it that sustains you? Hope?

Excess of being wells up in my heart.

And I weep—for the child in the womb
who has blossomed in a cage of darkness,
for the mother without breasts or arms,
for the unrepentant father hiding in the wings of your undoing,
for the future which is aftertaste,
and the death that will leave none of us alone.

Who has not sat, scared, before his heart's curtain?

One on each side of barred glass,
we approached each other warily at first
across a vast and ignorant yearning.
Now we know each other well.
Although to the patroller, with his clanking keys
and dull observing eye, not a thing has changed.

Who has turned us around like this, so that
whatever we do, we always have the aspect
of one who leaves?

Misery still oozes through the walls
like sewage into a contaminated well,
and humming over everything like fear
is fear. And yet there is that oldest of joys—
there is you telling me a joke, and
there is me laughing.

❧❧❧

Sarah Collins Honenberger, of Tappahannock, writes:

While "An Innocent in the House of the Dead" is not a joyful poem, I have selected it because it pushes me to be a better writer and a better person.

The author, Joanna Catherine Scott, is a North Carolina poet and world traveler, who has experienced more pain and joy than most people. She uses her imagination to fuel an inspiring empathy for others, and she uses her words to open those windows to the rest of us.

This poem speaks to me not only as a fiction writer, but also as a citizen of the global community. As a catalyst, the poem compels me to explore more deeply the thoughts and emotions of characters whose paths diverge from my life experience. It reminds me to focus on the details, but it won't let me forget that observation alone is insufficient unless the exploration uncovers the less easily discerned resonance of our shared humanity. Writing and reading can bring us closer together. Now more than ever with world peace threatened by fanatics, we need to find and celebrate the universality in different cultures and lifestyles.

A Ritual to Read to Each Other

William Stafford

If you don't know the kind of person I am
and I don't know the kind of person you are
a pattern that others made may prevail in the world
and following the wrong god home we may miss our star.

For there is many a small betrayal in the mind,
a shrug that lets the fragile sequence break
sending with shouts the horrible errors of childhood
storming out to play through the broken dyke.

And as elephants parade holding each elephant's tail,
but if one wanders the circus won't find the park,
I call it cruel and maybe the root of all cruelty
to know what occurs but not recognize the fact.

And so I appeal to a voice, to something shadowy,
a remote important region in all who talk:
though we could fool each other, we should consider—
lest the parade of our mutual life get lost in the dark.

For it is important that awake people be awake,
or a breaking line may discourage them back to sleep;
the signals we give—yes or no, or maybe—
should be clear: the darkness around us is deep.

❧❧❧

Thayer Cory, of Williamsburg, writes:

In my professional role as a psychotherapist, I see people every day who are driven by the universal longing for meaningful relationships. This longing pulls us, often in conflicting directions, into fighting wars (both public and private) and working for peace. I'm aware of the many betrayals, large and small, which break the fragile threads that bind people together.

In "A Ritual To Read To Each Other," William Stafford eloquently reminds us that we live in a sacred but fragile universe that can be sustained only by conscious connectedness. We create those bonds by understanding the errors of our imperfect histories, by facing our foibles, and by choosing to reach out to others. In short, we must know who we are. Only then can we honor our differences and embrace the fact that we live in a world of interdependence.

As a Quaker, I believe there is a divine spark in every person. Stafford begs us to wake up to it, tells us that without its guidance we will get lost in the dark.

It's easy to fall asleep; there are so many ways to disengage, to hide behind the wall of denial and fear where cruelty and isolation take hold. We live in a world where that remote, important region — the soul — is often in the shadows of our awareness. This poem calls us to lift the veil.

The darkness around us is deep. The island of light that grows with expanding consciousness and genuine connectedness is our only hope.

Ulysses

Alfred, Lord Tennyson

It little profits that an idle king,
By this still hearth, among these barren crags,
Match'd with an aged wife, I mete and dole
Unequal laws unto a savage race,
That hoard, and sleep, and feed, and know not me.
I cannot rest from travel: I will drink
Life to the lees: All times I have enjoy'd
Greatly, have suffer'd greatly, both with those
That loved me, and alone, on shore, and when
Thro' scudding drifts the rainy Hyades
Vext the dim sea: I am become a name;
For always roaming with a hungry heart
Much have I seen and known; cities of men
And manners, climates, councils, governments,
Myself not least, but honour'd of them all;
And drunk delight of battle with my peers,
Far on the ringing plains of windy Troy.
I am a part of all that I have met;
Yet all experience is an arch wherethro'
Gleams that untravell'd world whose margin fades
For ever and forever when I move.
How dull it is to pause, to make an end,
To rust unburnish'd, not to shine in use!
As tho' to breathe were life! Life piled on life
Were all too little, and of one to me
Little remains: but every hour is saved
From that eternal silence, something more,
A bringer of new things; and vile it were
For some three suns to store and hoard myself,
And this gray spirit yearning in desire
To follow knowledge like a sinking star,
Beyond the utmost bound of human thought.

This is my son, mine own Telemachus,
To whom I leave the sceptre and the isle,—
Well-loved of me, discerning to fulfil
This labour, by slow prudence to make mild
A rugged people, and thro' soft degrees
Subdue them to the useful and the good.
Most blameless is he, centred in the sphere
Of common duties, decent not to fail
In offices of tenderness, and pay
Meet adoration to my household gods,
When I am gone. He works his work, I mine.

There lies the port; the vessel puffs her sail:
There gloom the dark, broad seas. My mariners,
Souls that have toil'd, and wrought, and thought with me—
That ever with a frolic welcome took
The thunder and the sunshine, and opposed
Free hearts, free foreheads—you and I are old;
Old age hath yet his honour and his toil;
Death closes all: but something ere the end,
Some work of noble note, may yet be done,
Not unbecoming men that strove with Gods.
The lights begin to twinkle from the rocks:
The long day wanes: the slow moon climbs: the deep
Moans round with many voices. Come, my friends,
'Tis not too late to seek a newer world.
Push off, and sitting well in order smite
The sounding furrows; for my purpose holds
To sail beyond the sunset, and the baths
Of all the western stars, until I die.
It may be that the gulfs will wash us down:
It may be we shall touch the Happy Isles,
And see the great Achilles, whom we knew.
Tho' much is taken, much abides; and tho'
We are not now that strength which in old days

Moved earth and heaven, that which we are, we are;
One equal temper of heroic hearts,
Made weak by time and fate, but strong in will
To strive, to seek, to find, and not to yield.

❦❦❦

Jim Izzo, of Toano, writes:

I first encountered Tennyson's "Ulysses" as a college freshman, one of the first turning points in my life. This poem was an ironic choice at my age (I was nineteen then) because it focuses on a much older man looking back on his life, trying to decide what to do with the rest of it. I was most impressed with its final line: "To strive, to seek, to find, and not to yield," because I viewed those words as a challenge to all young people. Those words, as well as "I will drink/ Life to the lees," became my goal and inspiration.

I returned to "Ulysses" several years later when I began teaching British literature to high school students. Still close to their age, I showed them how it speaks to young adults.

When I retired several years ago, after thirty-five years of teaching, there was an emptiness in my life that only meaningful work could fill. I "sought and found" three part-time jobs: teaching adults was followed by freelance journalism, which was followed by supervising student teachers in the graduate program of a local college. Like Ulysses, I knew that "Some work of noble note, may yet be done," and that "Old age hath yet his honour and his toil." Like Ulysses, I was not content "To rust unburnish'd." I decided to undertake a new journey.

Thus, "Ulysses," to which I return when confronting life's various challenges, continues to re-energize me today. It will always be my nearest poem.

Do Not Go Gentle Into That Good Night

Dylan Thomas

Do not go gentle into that good night,
Old age should burn and rave at close of day;
Rage, rage against the dying of the light.

Though wise men at their end know dark is right,
Because their words had forked no lightning they
Do not go gentle into that good night.

Good men, the last wave by, crying how bright
Their frail deeds might have danced in a green bay,
Rage, rage against the dying of the light.

Wild men who caught and sang the sun in flight,
And learn, too late, they grieved it on its way,
Do not go gentle into that good night.

Grave men, near death, who see with blinding sight
Blind eyes could blaze like meteors and be gay,
Rage, rage against the dying of the light.

And you, my father, there on the sad height,
Curse, bless, me now with your fierce tears, I pray.
Do not go gentle into that good night.
Rage, rage against the dying of the light.

Esther Whitman Johnson, of Roanoke, writes:

I've carried this poem with me since I encountered it in a college anthology. "Rage, rage against the dying of the light." — Has there ever been a stronger call to live every day as if it were your last?

My North Dakota grandparents lived into their nineties, carrying their pioneer, homesteading spirit with them until the end. Strong, hardy, healthy, independent. My father-in-law, a World War I veteran, lived to be one-hundred and five. The DMV renewed his driver's license for seven years at age ninety-nine. My mother died at ninety-five, and even in dementia she walked, laughed, and carried herself as she had when she was a WAVE in World War II.

In the past decade, in my fifties and sixties, I've begun raging myself. I've traveled the globe, often by myself, taught English in China and Europe, participated with Habitat for Humanity in building houses from Madagascar to Vietnam, from Nicaragua to Cambodia. I've taken a freighter to the fiords of Patagonia and a sleeper train across central China. I've learned a new language and immersed myself with local families in five Latin American countries. Yes, we all die, but we can do so much until then. At age sixty-six, I'll be in the Gobi Desert raging against the night from atop a camel. Join me and we'll rage together!

The Hound of Heaven
(Stanza 1)

Francis Thompson

I fled Him, down the nights and down the days;
  I fled Him, down the arches of the years;
I fled Him, down the labyrinthine ways
  Of my own mind; and in the midst of tears
I hid from Him, and under running laughter.
      Up vistaed hopes I sped;
      And shot, precipitated,
Adown Titanic glooms of chasmèd fears,
  From those strong Feet that followed, followed after.
      But with unhurrying chase,
      And unperturbèd pace,
Deliberate speed, majestic instancy,
     They beat—and a Voice beat
     More instant than the Feet—
'All things betray thee, who betrayest Me.'

Monsignor William H. Carr, of Richmond, writes:

I would like to offer "The Hound of Heaven" as a nearest poem; the opening stanza in particular stirred my interest in the rest of the poem. In these lines, we see God's child fleeing God and God's "unhurrying chase," which right away gives me confidence that God will find me when I stray.

Francis Thompson's example offers me hope. I learned that he had a difficult life; yet, he was still able to write about God's passion for His children. His great work is realistic and consoling.

Sadiq

Brian Turner

It is a condition of wisdom in the archer to be patient
because when the arrow leaves the bow, it returns no more.
Sa'di

It should make you shake and sweat,
nightmare you, strand you in a desert
of irrevocable desolation, the consequences
seared into the vein, no matter what adrenaline
feeds the muscle its courage, no matter
what god shines down on you, no matter
what crackling pain and anger
you carry in your fists, my friend,
it should break your heart to kill.

John M. Koelsch, of Salem, writes:

Brian Turner's book of poetry HERE, BULLET is a compelling picture of the current wars in the Mideast and of war overall. His poem "Sadiq" is the nearest to me because it reflects what I know to be the real tragedy of war from my own experiences as a combat platoon leader in Vietnam. I have never seen it expressed more succinctly and with such clarity.

So close is the poem to me that I recited it in the Solo Dramatic Poetry Category for the 2012 National Veterans Creative Arts Festival. The presentation was awarded a Silver Medal for second place at the National level.

As toilsome I wander'd Virginia's woods

Walt Whitman

As toilsome I wander'd Virginia's woods,
To the music of rustling leaves kick'd by my feet, (for 'twas
      autumn,)
I mark'd at the foot of a tree the grave of a soldier;
Mortally wounded he and buried on the retreat, (easily all
could I understand,)
The halt of a mid-day hour, when up! no time to lose—yet
      this sign left,
On a tablet scrawl'd and nail'd on the tree by the grave,
Bold, cautious, true, and my loving comrade.

Long, long I muse, then on my way go wandering,
Many a changeful season to follow, and many a scene of life,
Yet at times through changeful season and scene, abrupt,
alone, or in the crowded street,
Comes before me the unknown soldier's grave, comes the
      inscription rude in Virginia's woods,
Bold, cautious, true, and my loving comrade.

James McNally, of Norfolk, writes:

As is the case with most Virginians, I am taken up with history, but strangely, when I approach or walk around Williamsburg, my mind lingers on the surrounding woods more than on the historical structures.

I have been wandering through woods and parks all my life. When I was ten years old, the family moved from the maple-shaded streets of Ballston to across the streetcar track from a wooded slope below Fort Myer, just around the corner from Arlington National Cemetery. I spent many afternoons among the tall oaks and hickories, sycamores and beeches, shuffling the leaves. The family farm in Fairfax, chimney clapboard with house-wide porch, had its garden, orchard, barn, pasture, and cornfield surrounded by second-growth trees, which I explored in many ways.

My woodsy background undoubtedly contributed to the resounding impression made on me by "As toilsome I wander'd Virginia's woods," met in the tenth grade when I made a bet I could read all of LEAVES OF GRASS. The poem is, for me, history at first hand. "Toilsome" made me feel I was doing something more than loafing my soul in the woods. "I mark'd at the foot of a tree the grave of a soldier," with its repeated epitaph "Bold, cautious, true, and my loving comrade," became a criterion for my judgment of character, of course with uneven results. The "inscription rude" remains inscribed in my mind.

Meet the Poets

Anna Akhmatova (1889-1966) was a Russian modernist poet. Among her best-known works are *Requiem* (published posthumously) and *Poem Without a Hero*, both written as reactions to the horror of the Stalinist Terror.

Margaret Atwood (1939-) is a Canadian poet, novelist, literary critic, essayist, and environmental activist. A prolific novelist, she is also the author of twenty poetry collections, including *Eating Fire: Selected Poems, 1965-1995* (UK,1998) and most recently, *The Door* (2007).

Joseph F. Awad (1929-2009) was a poet, painter, and business executive. He served as Virginia's Poet Laureate from 1998 to 2000. His best-known poetry collection is *Leaning To Hear the Music*. His poetry has been anthologized with both Arab-American and Irish-American writers.

Kristin Berkey-Abbott (1965-) earned a Ph.D. from the University of South Carolina and now oversees the General Education Department at the Art Institute of Ft. Lauderdale. She has published two poetry collections, *Whistling Past the Graveyard* and *I Stand Here Shredding Documents*, and is working on her first full-length book. Her website, with connections to her blogs, is www.kristinberkey-abbott.com.

William Blake (1757-1827) was an English poet, painter, and printmaker, considered a seminal figure in the history of the poetry and visual arts of the Romantic Age. Among his best-known works are the illuminated texts of *Songs of Innocence, The Marriage of Heaven and Hell*, and *Jerusalem: The Emanation of the Giant Albion*.

Christopher John Brennan (1870-1932) was an Australian poet. His major publication is *Poems* (1914), a quest narrative, autobiographical in nature, showing the persona's pursuit of Eden. It is a collection of poems conceived as a whole, although each poem can be read individually.

Rupert Brooke (1887-1915) was an English poet best known for his war sonnets written during World War I, particularly "The Soldier," which was read from the pulpit of St. Paul's Cathedral on Easter Sunday, three weeks before the poet's death. His collection *1914 & Other Poems* was published later that year.

Lewis Carroll (1832-1898) was an English writer, mathematician, Anglican deacon, and photographer. His most famous writings are *Alice's Adventures in Wonderland* and its sequel *Through the Looking-Glass,* as well as the poems "The Hunting of the Snark" and "Jabberwocky," all examples of the literary nonsense genre.

Constantine Cavafy (1863-1933) was a Greek poet who lived in Alexandria and worked as a journalist and civil servant. Almost all of Cavafy's work was in Greek; yet his poetry remained unrecognized in Greece until after the publication of his first anthology *Poiçmata (Poems)* in 1935.

G. K. Chesterton (Gilbert Keith Chesterton, 1874-1936), known as a master of paradox, was a prolific English writer of fantasy, Christian apologetics, mystery, literary criticism, and poetry. Among his many works are *Orthodoxy* and *The Everlasting Man*. He created the figure of Father Brown in a series of detective stories.

Lucille Clifton (1936-2010) was an American writer and educator who served as Poet Laureate of Maryland from 1979 to 1985. She published numerous children's books and thirteen poetry collections, most notably *Blessing The Boats: New and Collected Poems 1988-2000*, winner of the National Book Award.

Samuel Taylor Coleridge (1772-1834) was an English poet, literary critic, and philosopher, co-founder (with William Wordsworth) of the Romantic Movement in England and a member of the Lake Poets. He wrote the poems "The Rime of the Ancient Mariner" and "Kubla Khan," as well as the major prose work *Biographia Literaria*. His critical writings helped introduce German idealist philosophy to English-speaking culture.

Billy Collins (1941-) served as Poet Laureate of the United States from 2001 to 2003. He is a Distinguished Professor at Lehman College, New York, and Senior Distinguished Fellow of the Winter Park Institute, Florida. He has published fourteen poetry collections, most recently *Horoscopes for the Dead* (2011).

George Cooper (1840-1927) studied law, but after practicing for a short time, he renounced his profession to devote himself to writing. He is best remembered for his children's poems, many of them collected in *School and Home Melodies*, and for a volume of hymns titled *The Chaplet*.

Stephen Crane (1871-1900) was an American author. Prolific throughout his short life, he wrote notable works in the Realist tradition, as well as early examples of American Naturalism and Impressionism. His best known works are *The Red Badge of Courage* and his short story "The Open Boat."

E. E. Cummings (Edward Estlin Cummings, 1894-1962) was an American poet, painter, essayist, author, and playwright. His body of work encompasses approximately 2,900 poems, two autobiographical novels, four plays, and several essays, as well as numerous drawings and paintings.

Emily Dickinson (1830-1886) was born and lived all of her life in Amherst, Massachusetts. She wrote approximately 1,800 poems, most of which were published posthumously. Her brief, lyrically intense works, written in her inimitable signature style, have made her iconic and beloved in American letters.

John Donne (1572-1631) was an English poet, satirist, and lawyer and a cleric in the Church of England, often considered the pre-eminent representative of the metaphysical poets. Most of his poems were published posthumously, with the exception of *Anniversaries* and *Devotions upon Emergent Occasions*.

Michael Drayton (1563-1631) was born in Warwickshire, England, and came to literary prominence during the Elizabethan era. A prolific writer whose work was published widely during his lifetime, he is best known for his historical poems, notably "The Ballad of Agincourt."

T. S. Eliot (Thomas Stearns Eliot, 1888-1965) is considered one of the 20th century's major poets. Born in the United States, he moved to Great Britain and became a naturalized British subject. A social and literary critic and a master of the Modernist literary movement, he was awarded the Nobel Prize for Literature in 1948.

Ralph Stillman Emerson (1907- ?), a native New Englander, was born in Chelsea, Massachusetts, and lived in Everett, near Boston, most of his life. He followed music as a profession for a number of years, but began writing poetry in 1938. Having had no formal guidance in creative writing, he wrote as an avocation.

Ralph Waldo Emerson (1803-1882) was an American essayist, lecturer, and poet, who led the Transcendentalist movement in the mid-19th century. Seen as a champion of individualism, he disseminated his thoughts through published essays and more than 1,500 public lectures across the United States.

Louise Erdrich (1954-) is an American novelist and poet whose work often features Native American characters and settings. She is a member of the Turtle Mountain Band of Chippewa Indians, a band of the Anishinaabe. In 2012, she received the National Book Award for Fiction for her novel *The Round House*.

Terri Kirby Erickson (1958-), a widely published North Carolina poet, is the author of four poetry collections, including *In the Palms of Angels*, which was a Finalist for Poetry in the 2013 International Book Awards, winner of a Nautilus Silver Award for Poetry, and a Gold Medal for Poetry in the Next Generation Indie Book Awards.

Eugene Field (1850-1895) was an American journalist, social critic, and poet born in St. Louis, Missouri, and best known for his children's poetry and humorous essays. Many of his works were accompanied by paintings from Maxfield Parrish.

Robert Frost (1874-1963) was an American poet, highly regarded for his realistic depictions of rural life and his command of American vernacular. He often employed rural settings in his work, using them to examine complex social and philosophical themes. He published twenty-six poetry collections and received four Pulitzer Prizes for Poetry, among many other awards. He is one of America's best-loved poets.

Nikki Giovanni (1943-) is an American writer, critic, and educator. She has published some twenty poetry books, as well as numerous children's stories. She was nominated for the Grammy Award for Best Spoken Word Album for her album *The Nikki Giovanni Poetry Collection*. She is a University Distinguished Professor at Virginia Tech.

Edgar Guest (1881-1959), a prolific English-born American poet, was widely read in the first half of the 20th century and at times referred to as the "People's Poet." He wrote thousands of poems, which were syndicated in some three hundred newspapers and collected in over twenty books. He served as Poet Laureate of Michigan.

John Haines (1924-2011) was an American poet and educator. He was born in Virginia but lived in Alaska most of his life, and he served as that state's Poet Laureate. He published nine collections of poetry, notably *Winter Light* and *For the Century's End: Poems 1990-1999*.

Cathryn Hankla (1958-), a native of Southwest Virginia, is the author of eleven books of poetry and fiction, including *Last Exposures: A Sequence of Poems*. A PEN Syndicated fiction prize winner and Virginia Commission Fellow, she publishes regularly in literary journals and anthologies and edits poetry for *The Hollins Critic*. She is the Susan Gager Jackson Professor of Creative Writing at Hollins University.

Joy Harjo (1951-) is a Native American poet, musician, and author. She is a member of the Muscogee (Creek) Nation and is of Cherokee descent. She has published numerous books of poetry and has received the Lifetime Achievement Award from the Native Writers' Circle of the Americas. She teaches at the University of Illinois.

Robert Hayden (1913-1980) was an American poet, essayist, and educator. He published several collections of poetry, notably *Words in the Mourning Time* and *Angle of Ascent*. He was appointed Consultant in Poetry to the Library of Congress in 1976, the first African-American to hold that position.

Felicia Dorothea Hemans (1793-1835) was an English poet, widely read during her lifetime. Although her popularity declined as she came to be seen primarily as a children's poet, her work has experienced a critical reassessment in recent years and is once more finding its way into anthologies and literary collections.

Jane Hirshfield (1953-) is an American poet, essayist, and translator. She has published seven books of poetry and several translations of Japanese verse. In 1979, Hirshfield received lay ordination in Soto Zen at the San Francisco Zen Center. In 2012, she was elected a Chancellor of the Academy of American Poets.

Gerard Manley Hopkins (1844-1889) was an English poet, Roman Catholic convert, and Jesuit priest, whose posthumous fame established him among the leading Victorian poets. His experimental explorations in prosody and his use of imagery established him as a bold innovator at a time of largely traditional verse.

Langston Hughes (1902-1967) was an American poet, social activist, novelist, playwright, and columnist. He was one of the earliest innovators of the then-new literary art form "jazz poetry" and is best known as a leader of the Harlem Renaissance.

Julie Ellinger Hunt (1979-) is a Pushcart-nominated writer and artist from New Jersey. Her work can be seen in numerous anthologies and publications, including *NYQ, Blazevox, Forge Journal* , and *Virgogray Press*. She has also published two full collections of poetry, *Ever Changing* and *In New Jersey*.

James Henry Leigh Hunt (1784-1859), best known as Leigh Hunt, was an English critic, essayist, and poet. His *Poetical Works* in two volumes, which he revised himself, were printed in Boston in 1857, and another edition (London and New York) by his son, Thornton Hunt, appeared in 1860.

Richard Jones (1953-) is a London-born American poet and the author of seven poetry books, most recently *The Correct Spelling & Exact Meaning*, as well as several limited-edition volumes. He is currently Professor of English at DePaul University in Chicago.

A.M. Juster (1956-) is an American poet and translator, the author of four books: *The Secret Language of Women, Laura, The Satires of Horace*, and most recently, *Tibullus' Elegies* by Oxford University Press. His translations of Aldhelm's *Riddles* and Maximianus's *Elegies* should be available in late 2014 or early 2015.

Rudyard Kipling (1865-1936) was an English short-story writer, poet, and novelist, often remembered for his tales and poems about British soldiers in India and his children's stories. In 1907 he was awarded the Nobel Prize in Literature, the first English-language writer to receive the prize. He was offered the British Poet Laureateship, but declined.

Nagase Kiyoko (1906-1995) was a Japanese poet who never considered herself a professional writer. She published her first book of poems at the age of 24 and her 12th book in the year she died. Empress Michiko of the Japanese royal family translated one of Kiyoko's poems into English: "O You Who Come to Me at Dawn."

Gerrit Komrij (1944-2012) was a Dutch poet, novelist, translator, critic, journalist, and playwright. One of his country's leading writers and literary critics, he was awarded some of the nation's highest literary awards, including the P. C. Hooft Award. He was Poet Laureate of the Netherlands from 2000 to 2004.

Maxine Kumin (1925-) is an American poet and author. The recipient of numerous awards for her work, she served as Poet Laureate of the United States from 1981 to 1982. She is the author of seventeen poetry collections, six novels, and numerous children's books.

Charles Lamb (1775-1834) was an English essayist, best known for his *Essays of Elia* and for the children's book *Tales from Shakespeare*, which he produced with his sister, Mary Lamb, who lived under his care. He worked as a clerk for the East India Company, while doubling as a writer, throughout most of his life.

Philip Larkin (1922-1985) was an English poet and novelist, as well as a jazz critic for *The Daily Telegraph* from 1961 to 1971. He received numerous honors for his work, including the Queen's Gold Medal for Poetry. Among his best-known collections published during his lifetime are *The Whitsun Weddings* and *High Windows*.

Dorianne Laux (1952-) is an American poet born in Augusta, Maine. She is a professor at North Carolina State University's creative writing program and in the MFA Writing Program at Pacific University. She is the author of seven poetry collections, most recently *The Book of Women*.

Edward Lear (1812-1888) was an English artist, illustrator, author, and poet, best known for his literary nonsense in poetry and prose and especially his limericks. He popularized the form, most notably through his volume *A Book of Nonsense*, which went through several editions during his lifetime.

Henry Wadsworth Longfellow (1807-1882) was an American poet and educator whose works include "Paul Revere's Ride," "The Song of Hiawatha," and "Evangeline." One of the five Fireside Poets, he was also the first American to translate Dante Alighieri's *The Divine Comedy*.

John Masefield (1878-1967) was an English poet and writer and was Poet Laureate of the United Kingdom from 1930 until his death. A prolific writer, he is often remembered as the author of the classic children's novels *The Midnight Folk* and *The Box of Delights*, as well as memorable poems, including "The Everlasting Mercy" and "Sea-Fever."

Kindra M. McDonald (1978-) graduated from Virginia Wesleyan College and received her MFA in poetry from Queens University of Charlotte. She teaches Introduction to Poetry at The Muse Writers Center and is co-founder and editor of Copaiba Press. Her work has appeared in various journals.

Jim Wayne Miller (1936-1996), a North Carolina native, wrote his first book of poetry, *Copperhead Cane*, while a graduate student at Vanderbilt, where he studied with the poet Donald Davidson, who encouraged him to write about his mountain home. Miller's book is credited, by critic Fred Chappell, with beginning the "Appalachian Literary Movement" and influencing a generation of Appalachian writers.

A. A. Milne (Alan Alexander Milne, 1882-1956) was an English poet, novelist, and playwright, best known for his books about the teddy bear Winnie-the-Pooh and for various children's poems. Among his numerous plays are *Toad of Toad Hall*, an adaptation of *The Wind in the Willows*.

Moondog (Louis Thomas Hardin, 1916-1999) was a blind American composer, musician, poet, and inventor of several musical instruments. Moving to New York as a young man, Moondog made a deliberate decision to make his home on the streets, where he spent approximately twenty of the thirty years he lived in the city.

Lisel Mueller (1924-) is a German-born American poet. She is the author of eleven poetry books and several volumes of translation. Among the recognitions she has received for her work are the National Book Award in Poetry, for *The Need to Hold Still*, and a Pulitzer Prize in Poetry, for *Alive Together: New and Selected Poems.*

Giavanna Munafo (1961-), whose poems have appeared in various journals, teaches at Dartmouth College, where she served also as the director of the Center for Women & Gender, and then as the director for training and educational programs in the Office of Institutional Diversity & Equity. She lives in Norwich, Vermont, with her partner Jim Walsh, and their son, Max.

Ogden Nash (1902-1971) was an American poet well known for his light verse. He wrote over five hundred pieces of comic verse and gained renown very early in his career, with his first collection titled *Hard Lines*. The best of his work was published in fourteen volumes between 1931 and 1972.

John Shaw Neilson (1872-1942) was an Australian poet who worked as a manual laborer in rural Victoria and South Wales for much of his life, while practicing his craft. His first poetry collection was *Heart of Spring*, after which he published four other books, including *Beauty Imposes: Some Recent Verse.*

Alfred Noyes (1880-1958) was an English poet, best known for his ballads "The Highwayman" and "The Barrel-Organ." In a nationwide poll conducted by the BBC in 1995 to find Britain's favorite poems, "The Highwayman" was ranked 15th.

Naomi Shihab Nye (1952-) is a poet, songwriter, and novelist. She was born to a Palestinian father and an American mother. Although she regards herself as a "wandering poet," she refers to San Antonio as her home. She is the author of nine poetry collections and, most recently, a young-adult novel titled *Habibi*.

Gregory Orr (1947-) is an American poet and the author of numerous collections, most recently *River Inside the River: Poems*. He has received various awards for his work, notably the Award in Literature of the American Academy of Arts and Letters. He teaches at the University of Virginia, where he founded the MFA Program in Writing.

Sarah Dunning Park (1980-) is an American poet and artist. Her first collection of poetry is *What It Is Is Beautiful: Honest Poems for Mothers of Small Children*. She serves as poet-in-residence at the popular blog SimpleMom.net.

Molly Peacock (1947-) is the award-winning author of six books of poetry, a memoir, and *How to Read a Poem and Start a Poetry Circle*. Born in Buffalo, New York, she is a dual American-Canadian citizen and now resides in Toronto. She is on the faculty of the Spalding University Low-Residency Master of Fine Arts program.

Jon Pineda (1971-) is an American poet, memoirist, and novelist. He is the author of the poetry collections *The Translator's Diary* and *Birthmark*, the memoir *Sleep in Me*, and the novel *Apology*. He teaches creative writing at the University of Mary Washington.

Li Po (Li Bai, 701-762) is one of the most acclaimed poets in the history of Chinese poetry and was active during the flourishing of Chinese poetry in the mid-Tang Dynasty. A prolific writer, he is recognized to have stretched the rules of versification of his time. Around a thousand poems attributed to him are extant today.

Edgar Allan Poe (1809-1849) was an American author, poet, editor, and literary critic. Best known for his tales of mystery and the macabre, he was one of the earliest American practitioners of the short story and is often considered the inventor of the detective fiction genre, contributing also to the new genre of science fiction.

Jessica Powers (Sister Miriam, 1905-1988) was an American poet and Carmelite nun. Born in Wisconsin, she spent some time in Chicago and New York before entering the Milwaukee community of the Carmel Mother of God in 1941. She received the habit of the Carmelites in 1942 and is the author of five poetry collections.

Lawrence Raab (1946-) is an American poet born in Massachusetts. He is the author of eight poetry collections, including *What we don't know about each other*, winner of the National Poetry Series Prize. He teaches at Williams College and lives in Williamstown, Massachusetts.

Born into a family of artists, **Rashani Réa** (1952?-) began writing poetry at the age of eight. A strong sense of social awareness has guided her exploration through the world of transpersonal psychology and is inseparable from her art. Today, she stewards the land and creates individual and group retreats at her home/sanctuary in Hawai'i.

Edwin Arlington Robinson (1869-1935) was an American poet from Maine. He was awarded the Pulitzer Prize for Poetry three times: in 1922 for his first *Collected Poems*, in 1925 for *The Man Who Died Twice*, and in 1928 for *Tristram*. During his later years he was a frequent summer resident at the McDowell Colony.

Edwin Romond (1949-) is the author of seven collections of poetry and winner of numerous awards. Most recently, he received the 2013 New Jersey Poetry Prize for his poem "Champion." He retired from a career as a schoolteacher in 2003 and now works in the poetry program of the Geraldine R. Dodge Foundation.

Carl Sandburg (1878-1967) was an American writer and editor, best known for his poetry. He was the recipient of three Pulitzer Prizes: two for his poetry and another for his biography of Abraham Lincoln. H. L. Mencken called Sandburg "indubitably an American in every pulse-beat."

May Sarton (Eleanore Marie Sarton, 1912-1995) was a Belgium-born American poet, novelist, and memoirist. She is highly respected not only for the quality of her many novels and poems, but also—and perhaps more—for her memoirs, particularly her best-selling *Journal of a Solitude, 1972-1973.*

Joanna Catherine Scott (1943-) is an Australian-American writer whose work draws its inspiration from the sufferings and triumphs of real people. A Woodrow Wilson Visiting Fellow, she has published five novels, a collection of Indochinese oral histories, and four prize-winning poetry collections.

William Shakespeare (1564-1616) was an English poet and playwright, widely regarded as the greatest writer in the English language and the world's pre-eminent dramatist. His plays have been translated into every major living language and are performed more often than those of any other playwright. He is often called England's national poet and the "Bard of Avon."

Robert Siegel (1939-2012), an American writer, was the author of nine books of poetry and fiction, including *A Pentecost of Finches: New and Selected Poems*. He taught at Dartmouth, Princeton, and Goethe University in Frankfurt, and for twenty-three years at the University of Wisconsin-Milwaukee.

William Stafford (1914-1993) was an American poet and the twentieth Consultant in Poetry to the Library of Congress. His first major collection of poetry, *Traveling Through the Dark*, appeared when he was forty-eight years old; it won the National Book Award for Poetry. He eventually published fifty-seven volumes of poetry and non-fiction.

Wallace Stevens (1879-1955) was an American poet, highly esteemed for the philosophical nature of his work. He spent most of his life as an executive for an insurance company, while publishing numerous poems and substantive poetry collections, including his *Collected Poems*, winner of the 1955 Pulitzer Prize for Poetry.

Robert Louis Stevenson (1850-1894) was a Scottish novelist, poet, and essayist. His most famous works are *Treasure Island, Kidnapped*, and *Strange Case of Dr Jekyll and Mr Hyde*. A literary celebrity during his lifetime, he now ranks among the twenty-six most translated authors in the world.

Sara Teasdale (1884-1933) was an American lyrical poet. She published ten poetry collections in her lifetime, among them *Flame and Shadow, Dark of the Moon*, and *Love Songs*, for which she was awarded the 1918 Pulitzer Prize, the first woman to be recognized in this manner.

Alfred, Lord Tennyson (1809-1892) was Poet Laureate of Great Britain and Ireland during much of Queen Victoria's reign and remains one of the most popular British poets. Much of his verse was based on classical themes, yet many of his phrases have become commonplace in contemporary English.

Hilary Tham (1946-2005) was born in Malaysia as the daughter of Chinese immigrants and emigrated to the United States in 1969. She was the author of nine books of poetry and a memoir. She said of herself: "My identity is trellised on Judeo-Western principles and ideals, but my roots delve deep in Chinese lore."

Ernest Lawrence Thayer ("Phin," 1863-1940) was an American writer and poet, born in Massachusetts, who wrote "Casey at the Bat," "the single most famous baseball poem ever written" according to the *Baseball Almanac*. He wrote it while working as humor columnist for the *San Francisco Examiner* and signed it "Phin."

Dylan Thomas (1914-1953) was a Welsh poet. Although writing exclusively in the English language, Thomas has been acknowledged as one of the most important Welsh poets of the 20th century. His last collection, *Collected Poems, 1934–1952*, published when he was thirty-eight, won the Foyle poetry prize.

Francis Thompson (1859-1907) was an English poet and ascetic. After college, he moved to London to become a writer, but was forced to live as a street vagrant for years. A married couple read his poetry, rescued him, and arranged for the publication of his first book, *Poems*, in 1893. He published three books of poetry and essays in his lifetime.

Marina Tsvetaeva (1892-1941) was a Russian and Soviet lyrical poet. Her work is considered among some of the greatest in 20th century Russian literature. She lived through and wrote of the Russian Revolution of 1917 and the Moscow famine that followed it.

Brian Turner (1967-) is an American poet, essayist, and professor. He won the 2005 Beatrice Hawley Award for his debut collection, *Here, Bullet,* the first of many awards and honors received for this group of poems about his experience as a soldier in the Iraq War.

Paul Verlaine (1844-1896) was á French poet associated with the Symbolist movement. He is considered one of the greatest representatives of the *fin de siècle* epoch in international and French poetry. His *Complete Works* are available in critical editions from the Bibliothèque de la Pléiade.

Derek Walcott (1930-) is a Saint Lucian poet and playwright, winner of the 1992 Nobel Prize in Literature. He is Professor of Poetry at the University of Essex. His works include the Homeric epic poem *Omeros,* often viewed as his major achievement. He has received a MacArthur Foundation "genius" award, among many other commendations.

Victoria White (1995-) lives in Stonington, Connecticut, and is a student at Milton Academy in Milton, Massachusetts. Her poetry has been published in the *Kenyon Review, Cargoes, The Adroit Journal,* and *Scholastic*'s 'Best Teen Writing of 2013.'

Mary Brent Whiteside (1882?-1962?) was an American poet of New England ancestry, born in the South. She received an honorary Doctor of Letters degree from Oglethorpe University. Her poems and stories appeared in numerous magazines. Among her book publications are *The Eternal Quest and Other Poems* and *Bill 'Possum: His Book.*

Walt Whitman (1819-1892) was an American poet, essayist, and journalist. A humanist, he was integral to the transition between Transcendentalism and Realism, and is among the most influential poets in the American canon, often called the father of free verse. His best-known work is his poetry collection *Leaves of Grass.*

William Carlos Williams (1883-1963) was an American poet closely associated with Modernism and Imagism. He was also a pediatrician and general practitioner of medicine. His major collections are *Spring and All, The Desert Music and Other Poems, Pictures from Brueghel and Other Poems,* and the five-volume work *Paterson.*

William Wordsworth (1770-1850) was a major English Romantic poet who, with Coleridge, helped to launch the Romantic Age in English literature with the 1798 joint publication *Lyrical Ballads.* His magnum opus is generally considered to be *The Prelude.* He was Britain's Poet Laureate from 1843 until his death.

William Butler Yeats (1865-1939) was an Irish poet, one of the foremost figures of 20th century literature. He was a driving force behind the Irish Literary Revival and one of the founders of the Abbey Theatre. In 1923 Yeats was awarded the Nobel Prize in Literature, the first Irishman so honored.

Meet the Readers

Angela Anselmo was born and lived in New York City and on Long Island. She earned a B.S. degree from Columbia University and an M.S. degree from Long Island University. Her career was in nursing and nursing education. She has been writing poetry for twenty years, and in retirement began taking literature classes. She is a volunteer guide at The Museums of Colonial Williamsburg.

Originally from Pakistan, **Arooba Ayaz** entered her senior year of high school in the fall of 2013. She enjoys all types of art and draws in her free time. Arooba classifies herself as a pacifist and a feminist, and she aspires to be a psychologist and make the world a better place.

A bookseller for thirty years, **Bill Ayres** loves his job. He affirms, unequivocally, that he has "the best wife and family in the world" and has written "some good poems and two very bad novels." You may hear him knocking on your door, telling you to get out and vote. Otherwise, he enjoys food, music, church, kayaking... and feels "it is good to be Bill."

Carey K. Bagdassarian is a teacher and writer interested in the confluences of art and science. His scientific research has brought him, perhaps not too paradoxically, to a love for poetry.

Doris Baker, published poet, artist, traveler, and free-lance photographer, was Principal of an American Army Dependents School in Germany from 1950 until1980. She received a Master's degree from the University of Michigan and is the author of a novel, *The Originals*, about the Green Berets, and a nonfiction book, *I'll Let You Know When We Get There*.

Marie A. Barthelemy was born in the South of Belgium to a large, vibrant Catholic family. She studied nursing in Brussels, then pursued an advanced nursing degree in Richmond, Virginia, and is presently working as a nurse practitioner in Williamsburg. She and her husband JF have three grown children.

Daryl Ann Beeghley resides in the scenic Blue Ridge Highlands town of Lebanon with her husband of thirty-six years, Jamie. Now that her three children are grown and married, and after investing twenty-five years as a home educator, she delights in the creative pursuits of writing, making music, and constructing recycled art.

Tom Berkey served forty-three years in the United States Civil Service. He worked for various agencies in the information technology (IT) fields and was the Senior Manager in charge of IT audits nationwide for the Farm Credit Administration. He was also a navigator in the US Air Force and retired after thirty years of service in the Air Force Reserve Intelligence Service.

Originally from California, **Wendy R. Blair** holds a Master's degree in acting and directing, having worn more hats than Bartholomew Cubbins. Her résumé includes actress, singer, director, waitress, cook, writer, landscaper, event planner, speaker, fundraiser, business executive, teacher, and witness preparation specialist. These escapades have helped to prepare her for her calling as owner/operator of the Rose Hill Bed and Breakfast in Roanoke.

Jessica Malicki Blaisus lives in Portsmouth and is the proud wife of a US Marine. She received her B.A. diploma from Cleveland State University and her M.Litt. degree in Shakespeare and Performance from Mary Baldwin College. Jessica is delighted to work for the Virginia Stage Company and enjoys martial arts, video games, and unusual novels.

Professional storyteller **Laura J. Bobrow** calls herself an author who talks out loud. In her lifetime Laura has been a magazine editor, folk singer, sculptor, painter, poet, and lyricist. In the manner of the old bards, Laura frequently makes use of rhyme in the tales she tells. Her website address is www.laurajbobrow.com.

William T. "Bill" Bolling is the 39th Lieutenant Governor of Virginia. A Republican, he was elected twice to the position, in both the 2005 and 2009 general elections. He is the first Lieutenant Governor in the Commonwealth, since Don Beyer, to serve two consecutive terms. He also served, previously, in the Senate of Virginia. Bolling is a Vice President with Riggs, Counselman, Michaels and Downes, an independent insurance agency.

Al C. Bradley was born in Abingdon, Virginia, in 1946. He graduated from Lynchburg College in 1968 and then served as City Planner for Abingdon and Washington County from 1972 to 2005, the year he retired. He lives in Abingdon with his wife Leslie.

Rachel Brandon is in the 7th grade. She is involved with her church youth group and enjoys soccer and piano, as well as all kinds of outdoor activities. Rachel has a black lab named Murphy, a leopard gecko named Penelope, and a few frogs and hermit crabs. She loves all animals very much!

John A. Bray retired from the New York Police Department as a lieutenant and practiced criminal defense law on Long Island for thirty years before moving to Williamsburg in 2005. He is the author of four novels, *Flags of Our Sons, Blue Heat, Home Front,* and *Broken Force,* all published by Endeavour Press of London.

Ronnie Brown is the Arts in Education Manager at Virginia Repertory Theatre in Richmond, Virginia, and the State Coordinator for Poetry Out Loud: National Recitation Competition.

Some days **Mary E. Burns** considers herself retired from an IT professional career. She has returned to the beautiful, verdant, little city where she grew up, and wonders whether she is spending too much time feeding birds. It seems she can't get enough of them after years of living in big-city apartments with only pigeon sightings. She hopes her cats don't mind.

Andrew Cain was born in the neighborhood of the Dismal Swamp and reared at its hem. After several unsuccessful attempts to obey the artistic imperative to change his life, he continues to work in telecommunications by rearranging lights on a screen to satisfy shareholder expectations. He remembers Phlebas, who once was handsome and tall, in the hope of forgetting the cry of gulls.

Jerry Caldwell lives in Roanoke County, Virginia, and has been a journalist for more than three decades. His work has earned several Murrow Awards, two Emmys, and a Peabody. He was introduced to the lyrics and music of Louis Thomas Hardin, a.k.a. "Moondog," while living in Brooklyn, New York, in the late 1970s.

Jack Callan is a father, grandfather, poet, carpenter, and artist from Norfolk, Virginia. He and his poet-wife, Judith Stevens, host poetry events and conduct weekly writing workshops with seniors at a retirement community in Virginia Beach. He enjoys hiking and kayaking the Little River in Floyd, Virginia, which inspires much of his poetry.

Monsignor William H. Carr was ordained in Sacred Heart Cathedral, Richmond, in 1969 and has served in Richmond, Virginia Beach, and Williamsburg. He enjoys bringing people together and has participated in several church building projects. Monsignor Carr appreciates poetry and history as well as classical music.

Chad Carter is a forty-two-year-old courier for the Central Rappahannock Regional Library system in Virginia. He indulges in a myriad of pop culture—comics, movies, Gold Medal genre paperbacks, 1950s robot toys—while wrestling with the new world of publishing to attain "novelist" stature, said novels to evoke the stark paperback originals of earlier decades. Or so the dream goes.

Laura L. Close has an MFA degree from George Mason University and is the author of *T Party*, published in 2012. She likes herbs and has an herb garden, which explains the title of her manuscript *The Sound and Sense of Leaves*, in search of a publisher. She teaches English at NOVA Community College and reads extensively, in hopes of writing her own great American novel.

Cameron Conaway is an award-winning poet, a former MMA (Mixed Martial Arts) fighter, and the Social Justice Editor at GoodMenProject.com.

Thayer Cory is a practicing psychotherapist, a Quaker, a mother and grandmother, an aspiring poet, and an avid hiker. In all these arenas, she searches for the threads that keep us connected to human relationships, to the natural world, and to the divine.

Carroll W. Dale is a former American football wide receiver. He played at Virginia Tech and was twice named a second-team All-American. During his NFL career, he played with the champion Packers in Super Bowls I and II. Dale has been inducted into the Virginia Sports Hall of Fame, Packers Hall of Fame, College Football Hall of Fame, and Southwest Virginia Museum Walk of Fame. He is Assistant Vice Chancellor for Athletic Development at UVa-Wise.

The **Rev. Elinor Ritchie Dalton, Ret**. grew up in Ewing, Virginia, with her parents, Hubert and Dora Ritchie, and her sister, Rita (now Seale). A graduate of Thomas Walker High School, she majored in Home Economics and English at Madison College (now JMU). Thirty years after college graduation, she received a Master of Divinity degree from Wesley Theological Seminary and served over fifteen years as a United Methodist pastor. Her son John and his wife Kristin have two children, Parker and Hayden.

Gillian Dawson grew up in England and came to America in 1965. She was hired by Colonial Williamsburg in 1984 as an Historical Interpreter and started writing humorous poems to read to her colleagues in the break rooms. She has attended two poetry writing classes and is a regular participant in a poetry workshop.

A longtime resident of Virginia, **Martha Dillard** is a painter and a lover of flowers, friends, family, mountains, and good words. Like Billy Collins, she has forgotten a thing or two along the way.

JoAnn Falletta, a classical musician and orchestral conductor, is Music Director of the Virginia Symphony Orchestra and Buffalo Philharmonic Orchestra, as well as artistic director of the Hawai'i Symphony Orchestra. Her recordings have earned two Grammy Awards and nine Grammy nominations. She served as a member of the National Council on the Arts from 2008 to 2012.

A retired teacher, **Beverly Foote** received a Master's degree from the Bread Loaf School of English, Middlebury College. Her book *Sheets and Other Poems* won a first-place Christian Choice Book Award. She also published *A Journey of the Heart* and *The Good Life*.

June Forte is a writer, photographer, and lecturer. Her love of poetry took root in the library shelves of her childhood and continues to thrive. She teaches a variety of communication courses at Northern Virginia Community College in Woodbridge.

Serena Fusek is a writer and poet, as well as a traveler, amateur photographer, and avid reader. Some of her favorite reading material is poetry, and she has many poems that she keeps near. She has published several chapbooks of poems and a full-length collection titled *Alphabet of Foxes*.

James F. Gaines is Professor of Modern Foreign Languages and Literatures at the University of Mary Washington, President of Riverside Writers, and Past President of the Virginia Writers Club. He has published a number of poetic and prose translations of French authors, as well as his own poetry. His most recent collection, to be published in 2014, is *Downriver Waltz*.

Stan Galloway teaches English at Bridgewater College, in Bridgewater, Virginia. He also writes and appreciates all things poetical.

Thomas Gardner is a Professor of English at Virginia Tech, where he teaches courses in Modern and Contemporary Poetry and Close Reading. His book on Emily Dickinson and contemporary writers titled *A Door Ajar* appeared in 2006. Most mornings he can be found running the Poverty Creek trail, just outside of Blacksburg.

Angela German is a reader, writer, educator, wife, and mother of beautiful boys Hayden and Wyatt. She appreciates the support of her husband Kyle as she embarks on her endeavors as Citywide Teacher of the Year in Virginia Beach City Public Schools, where she has worked the past thirteen years.

Kristy Feltenberger Gillespie is a school counselor at Marsteller Middle School in Bristow, Virginia. By nature, she's a short-story writer, but she also writes young-adult novels and occasional poems. Her writing/reading blog is Keep Calm and Write On, at www.kristyfgillespie.com.

Bill Glose is a former paratrooper, Gulf War veteran, and author of two poetry collections *The Human Touch* and *Half a Man*. In a 1,500-mile journey exploring Virginia on foot, Bill kissed a fawn on the lips, jumped from a cliff into a water-filled quarry, and stripped naked to help set the world skinny-dip record.

Floyd D. Gottwald, Jr., served as Director and Chief Executive Officer of Albemarle Corp., a global specialty chemical company, for many years, and he is currently Director Emeritus of the corporation. He is Trustee Emeritus of the University of Richmond and a distinguished member of numerous professional and philanthropic societies.

Erick Green is a 2013 graduate of Virginia Tech. During his senior year, playing point guard for the Hokie basketball team, he led Division I in scoring at 25 points per game and was designated ACC Player of the Year. Shortly after graduation, he was drafted by the Denver Nuggets, with whom he will embark on his NBA career.

Congressman H. Morgan Griffith has been the U.S. Representative for Virginia's 9th Congressional District since 2011. He is a member of the Republican party. The district takes in a large swath of southwestern Virginia, including the New River Valley. He was the Majority Leader of the Virginia House of Delegates, where he represented the 8th District, serving from 1994 until 2011.

Wheston Chancellor Grove is an anachronism. He was born in Northern California, just before the cusp of the electronic Niagara, and moved to the East Coast at thirteen. Photographer, painter, writer, he loves the mountains and his bilingual dachshund, Kleine Baum (Little Tree) Tuck. "All charm and grace have been lost to a bygone era," he says, "and with it the woman of my dreams." *Ashened Rapture* was published in 2011.

Warren Meredith Harris has been a college teacher, a stage director, and the editor of a literary review, and he has held three fellowships from the National Endowment for the Humanities. His poems have appeared in numerous periodicals, and some are collected in his book *The Night Ballerina: A Poem Sequence in Seven Parts*. He enjoys birding and painting.

Clay Harrison was an Army MP during the Vietnam era and a police officer in Tampa, Florida, for thirty years, focusing on crime scene investigations. While living in Tampa, he was a "poet in the schools." Clay has donated his poetry to Salesian Inspirational Books for over fifty years and has been a contributor to *Ideals* and many spiritual publications. He was the People's Choice winner of the 2013 *Daily Press* Poetry Contest.

Dr. Donna Price Henry is Chancellor of the University of Virginia's College at Wise. Previously, she spent sixteen years at Florida Gulf Coast University as a founding faculty member, Faculty Senate president, and Dean of the College of Arts and Sciences for eight years. She is married to Allen Henry, a pilot for Federal Express, and they have twin daughters, Jessie and Margaret.

Martha Moruza Hepler graduated from the College of William & Mary; she is a third-generation Army wife and mother of two young children. Along with chronicling their international adventures on her blog (www.thisisourgypsycamp.typepad.com), she is a church music, ornithology, and photography nerd.

In the fall of 2013, **Cašmir Hodge** entered her junior year at Appomattox Regional Governor's School for the Arts and Technology, where she is majoring in literary arts. She enjoys reading, writing, drawing, and playing one of her instruments. Her dream is to become a licensed psychologist with her own practice for troubled youth.

Linda Holtslander is the Programming Director for the Loudoun County Public Library. She has an M.L.S. degree from the University of California at Berkeley and a B.A. degree in Journalism from University of the Americas in Mexico City. She has been an Adjunct Professor at San Jose State University and the University of California. A Research Fulbright Scholar in Helsinki, Finland, from 2008-2009, she worked with the Helsinki City Library and their "Next Library" Initiative.

Sarah Collins Honenberger's best-selling novel *Catcher, Caught* appears nationally on high school reading lists and is a Pen/Faulkner Foundation selection for its Writers in Schools program. Her other award-winning novels are *White Lies: A Tale of Babies, Vaccines, and Deception* and *Waltzing Cowboys*.

Gillian Huang-Tiller is Associate Professor of English at the University of Virginia's College at Wise, where she teaches Modern American Literature, Modern and Contemporary Poetry, Asian-American Literature, Diasporic Literature, and Western Literary Traditions. She has published widely on E.E. Cummings and is on the editorial board of *SPRING: The Journal of the E. E. Cummings Society*. Currently she is completing a monograph on Cummings and the Sonnet, 1923-1963.

Jim Izzo is a retired teacher of literature and journalism who lives in Toano with his wife Joanne and their two cats, Emily and Chapin. A free-lance journalist, he has also written a collection of poetry and a novel, co-authored with Joanne. He enjoys theatre, music, and playing the piano.

Esther Whitman Johnson is a retired high school counselor and English teacher who now spends her time in the passionate pursuit of volunteer travel, happily traipsing the globe and writing about her jaunts. She has recently returned from Mongolia, where she completed her 12th international build with Habitat for Humanity.

Isaiah Johnson is a junior at Appomattox Regional Governor's School. He has interests in writing, reading long novels, and the internet. He also likes analyzing music for literary devices.

Jacqueline Jules is an award-winning poet and author of two dozen children's books. After a number of years as a teacher and librarian, Jacqueline left the school system to devote herself to writing full time. She remains forever in awe of elementary school educators. Her website is at www.jacquelinejules.com.

Senator Timothy "Tim" Kaine is the junior United States Senator from the Commonwealth of Virginia. He was elected to the Senate in 2012 and took office in 2013. A member of the Democratic party, he served as the 51st Chairperson of the Democratic National Committee from 2009 to 2011, as the 70th Governor of Virginia from 2006 to 2010, and as mayor of Richmond, Virginia, from 1998 to 2001.

Derek Kannemeyer was born in Cape Town, South Africa, and raised in London, England. He was educated at the Universities of London and Virginia and teaches French at St. Catherine's School in Richmond. His writing has appeared in scores of periodicals from *Fiction International* to *Rolling Stone*, and he is an officer of the Poetry Society of Virginia.

John M. Koelsch is a veteran of the Vietnam War and an award-winning poet. He is the author of *Mickey 6*, a novel that chronicles the struggles of leadership in war. He lives in Salem with his wife Nancy Wheeler.

Dr. Carolyn Kreiter-Foronda served as Virginia's Poet Laureate from 2006 to 2008. She has authored six poetry books and co-edited two anthologies. Her award-winning poems have been published widely in the United States and abroad. Carolyn currently serves as a Literary Arts Specialist for a Metrorail Public Art Project. An accomplished painter, sculptor, and educator, she teaches art-inspired writing workshops for the Virginia Museum of Fine Arts.

May-Lily Lee hosts *Virginia Conversations* on Virginia Public Radio and Radio IQ. For more than two decades she worked with The Community Idea Stations, where she was an Emmy-award-winning producer, host of *Virginia Currents*, and host of *Battle of the Brains*.

Edward W. Lull served as a Navy submarine officer in his first career and business executive in his second. His writing includes poetry and essays, with a primary focus on narrative poetry. He uses classic forms for much of his poetry and has recently published a handbook of poetic forms for aspiring poets.

English teaching has been at the core of **Christy Lumm**'s life in the U.S. and four overseas countries, where she taught in the international diplomatic schools. She has found that poetry teaching is an enigma to many English teachers in a sequential, logical world, but she sees it as a wonderful challenge. Borrowing from William Carlos Williams, she says "So much depends on looking at life as a poet, since life without poetry is unimaginable."

Michal Mahgerefteh is an award-winning poet and artist from Israel who has lived in Virginia since 1986. She is editor and publisher of the international magazine *Poetica*. Michal is the author of four poetry collections and is working on a group of poems to accompany her new series of mixed media art, to be exhibited in Virginia and Washington, D.C.

Patricia Policarpio Martin is a social science research analyst for the Office of Retirement Policy at the Social Security Administration. Her recent published work focuses on vulnerable populations, including demographic and economic characteristics of subgroup comparisons involving beneficiaries of the Social Security and Supplemental Security Income programs. When she's not working, she enjoys international travel.

Solomon McCray, III, is a senior at Lafayette High School. He has lived in James City County (Williamsburg) his whole life and couldn't be happier. He plans on majoring in business or physical therapy, while trying to pursue a future in baseball. Baseball has been a huge contributor to the person he is today, and in the 2012 season he led the greater Williamsburg area in hitting with a .462 average.

For most of her adult life, **Ann McDowell** lived in Alexandria with her husband Charley McDowell, a Washington correspondent for the *Richmond Times-Dispatch*. For twenty-three years, she had a studio in the Torpedo Factory Art Center in Alexandria, working as a photographer and painter. In 2009, they moved to the Atlantic Shores Community in Virginia Beach, for her husband's Alzheimer's disease. He died in 2010.

Dr. James McNally was born in Washington, D.C., in 1924 and grew up in Arlington, then partially rural. He attended Washington-Lee High, the United States Marines, and the University of Virginia. Thirty-five years a college English professor, he has been happy in marriage, parenthood, and hope.

Kathi Mestayer has lived in Atlanta, New Jersey, Chicago, Ithaca (NY), and James City County. Her mother was a post-WWII immigrant from Scotland and brought the A.A. Milne poems with her. Kathi can still hear her reading them with her fearsome brogue and silly sense of humor. Kathi is a naturalist, free-lance writer, and hearing-loss advocate.

Joan C. Meyer was brought up in the shadows of the Smithsonian Museums, in Washington, D.C., not far from the Embassy of Canada, a country where she would spend several summers. A lover of learning, bibliophile, bibliosopher, and bibliomaniac, she identifies with and has been called Hermione Granger, her heroine. She attends Cranbrook Kingswood School, her Hogwarts, and her *nom de plume*, online, is Signal Spells.

A widely published poet and scholar, **Felicia Mitchell** has resided in Washington County since moving to Virginia in 1987 to teach English and creative writing at Emory & Henry College. Her poem "Tumbling Creek" is included in the Poetry Society of Virginia Metrorail Public Art Project in northern Virginia.

Jehan Rahim Mondal says: "'At the touch of love everyone becomes a poet.' Plato knew the seed. My journey as a student through the heart of poetry has lit my life in ways I could only dream beforehand. It begins with the souls of two cities, a poetess, God and his children, and a well of sparkling sweat. Love blossoming is forever pink, its petals shining brightly the light within and above us."

A former teacher, **Susan Carter Morgan** now owns a writing studio, where she leads adult writing workshops and mentors young writers. She also works at Germanna Community College in marketing. She loves walking, and any view of a river, lake, or ocean will stop her in her tracks.

Shirley Walker Moseley was born in tobacco country, Vernon Hill, Virginia, and grew up in Newport News. She graduated from Averett College, Danville, with an Associate degree in Secretarial Science and worked with the first neurosurgeon on the Peninsula for thirty-eight years. She loves photography, especially of sunsets, as well as reading and (at times) cooking. She and her husband have traveled extensively since her retirement.

Linda Nash, the music chair for the National League of American Pen Women, is an internationally acclaimed singer/songwriter. She has published two CDs, *Consider the Lilies* and *The Lilies of the Field,* and two children's books, *The Legend of the Lilies* and *A Tale of Three Trees*. In 2013, the world premiere of her choral work *Agnus Dei* was performed at The Annunciation Catholic Church in Washington, D.C.

Cynthia Johnson Newlon is Director of the Writing Center and Instructor in English at the University of Virginia's College at Wise. A native of Southwest Virginia, Cynthia claims Lee County as the family birthplace. She is a Teacher Consultant with the Appalachian Writing Project, a member of the National Writing Project. She says, "I love the feel of words on my tongue and of the pencil in my hand, as the words come out of my mind and onto the paper."

Richard C. Nottingham lives in Free Union.

Stuart C. Nottingham, a retired health care professional, lives and writes in Alexandria. He is married to fellow poet Linda Nottingham.

Maureen Theresa O'Dea is a first-generation Irish-American who grew up in Queens, New York. She is a practicing physician in the Washington suburbs. Her lifelong passion for writing is supported by the intensity of her medical practice and the endless grist for the mill that her practice provides.

Adele Richards Oberhelman is a retired Executive Secretary/Administrative Assistant who has worked at the Aluminum Company of America, the U. S. Army Aviation Material Laboratories, and Anheuser-Busch, Inc. The mother of one son, a physicist and systems engineer, she is considered to be an excellent cook who enjoys entertaining. She is a member of the Heritage Humane Society Auxiliary, Hospice House Guild, and the James City County Poets.

David J. Partie is a college professor of English and Modern Languages. He earned a Ph.D. degree in Comparative Literature from the University of Southern California and an M.Div. degree from Talbot Theological Seminary in New Testament Studies. His interests are acting, writing fiction and poetry, traveling, playing music, writing songs, and working on behalf of the mentally ill.

As a rising senior at Norfolk Academy, **Maggie Pecsok** knows this year holds the promise of a college frenzy. Essay writing and interviews, though, will not get in the way of her extracurricular passions, which include drawing, painting, singing, and kayaking. At school, she also acts, sings, and dances in various productions.

Maria Perez-Barton is a radiation therapist with Bachelor's degrees in Health Science and History and a minor in English. In her spare time, she loves to travel around the country with her husband and two Corgis. She also enjoys reading the poetry of Emily Dickinson, Ambrose Bierce, and Samuel Beckett.

Nancy Powell has traveled around the world and has lived in England and Australia. Currently, when not at her day job as Executive Assistant to the President of a manufacturing company, she can be found at home by the Hampton River, where she writes. Her poems have appeared in numerous publications, and her collection *How Far is Ordinary* was issued in 2007. A second collection is forthcoming.

Rita Sims Quillen is an award-winning and widely published poet. Among her poetry collections are *Her Secret Dream, October Dusk,* and *Counting the Sums.* She is also the author of a book of essays titled *Looking for Native Ground: Contemporary Appalachian Poetry.* She lives and farms on Early Autumn Farm in Scott County, Virginia, and was a finalist for appointment as the Poet Laureate of Virginia for 2012-2014.

Suzanne Underwood Rhodes's most recent poetry collection is a chapbook, *Hungry Foxes.* She has four other published volumes of poetry and creative prose and teaches part time at a community college and the Muse Writing Center. She also works full time as Director of Public Affairs for the charity Mercy Medical Airlift. Hiking and birding with her husband, a photographer, are among her passions.

Keyada M. Richardson is a recent graduate of Virginia Commonwealth University with a Master of Teaching (Secondary English Education) degree. In 2011 she received a Bachelor of Arts degree in English from Virginia Tech. She is now a 9th and 10th grade English teacher with the Spotsylvania County Public Schools.

Sara M. Robinson, an award-winning poet, is the author of *Love Always, Hobby and Jessie,* a memoir, and *Two Little Girls in a Wading Pool,* a book of poems. A second collection, *Stones for Words,* will be released in 2014. Her poems have recently appeared in *The Blue Ridge Anthology 2013* and in *Piedmont Virginian.* She teaches in the UVA/OLLI program. Formerly in the minerals mining industry, Sara is a patent holder and now enjoys the reinvention of her writing.

Naomi Rodman is a rising junior Biochemistry student at Virginia Tech. Along with a love for science, she loves reading, music, and the arts. When she is not studying or in classes, she likes to spend as much of her time outdoors as possible, hiking, camping, or simply enjoying the great outdoors.

Tristan Rose is a thirty-year-old single father who recently returned to college. He obtained his Associate's degree in Liberal Arts and is currently working on his Bachelor's degree in English/Literature, with plans to pursue a Master's degree in English/Literature. He likes to read and write, specifically in the science fiction and fantasy genres. He also enjoys photography and learning about alternative lifestyles and subcultures, namely leather, cyber-goth, and punk, among others.

Mary-Grace Rusnak is a former home-school teacher turned student and writer. She is currently pursuing her B.S. degree in Psychology from the College of William and Mary. A 2012 Coca-Cola scholar and USA Today All-Virginia Community College Academic Team member, she has had poems published in *Channel Marker* and *Winged Nation.*

Evie Safran is a retired teacher still teaching part time. She is also a caterer who grows food and often cooks at a homeless shelter in Charlottesville. She is interested in early childhood education, issues of social justice, food, and nutrition. She hopes to keep working, walking, and writing poetry, "'til I'm all used up!"

Nathan Salle is a senior at Appomattox Regional Governor's School for the Arts and Technologies. He resides in Richmond with his parents and is an avid cyclist and tennis player. Nathan enjoys writing all genres of literature, especially poetry, which is his favorite. He would like to thank his poetry teacher Gail Giewont (Mrs. G) for making him do this as an assignment for class.

Christopher Scalia is an Associate Professor of English at the University of Virginia's College at Wise, where he teaches courses in British literature, composition, and creative writing. A native of McLean, he attended the College of William & Mary and earned his Ph.D. degree from the University of Wisconsin-Madison.

Sharron Singleton was a social worker assisting low-income families and the mentally ill and a community organizer around issues of civil rights and the anti-nuclear war movement, before devoting herself to poetry. Her work has appeared in numerous journals and has won several awards. Her chapbook *A Thin Thread of Water* was published in 2010. She is married, with children and grandchildren, teaches poetry, and loves to garden.

Barbara Drucker Smith is the author of *A Poetic Journey, Prose from the Old Century to the New,* and *Darling Loraine, the Story of A. Louis Drucker, A Grateful Jewish Immigrant.* She leads a monthly poetry group at the Peninsula Fine Arts Center in Newport News and is a member of the Christopher Newport Writers Conference Advisory Board, as well as other professional and artistic societies. She is an improvisational pianist, a swimmer, a hand-blown glass sculptor, and a world traveler.

Deborah Mallett Spanich is registrar at a small art museum, board member of the Anne Spencer House and Garden Museum, and Western Region VP of the Poetry Society of Virginia. Her poetry chapbook is titled *Morning Bread.* She loves books, tea, yoga, and coffee, and fondly remembers that her father always believed in her.

Christine Sparks was born and raised in a home filled with music and books. When she was ten, one of her poems was featured on television, an experience she has never forgotten. An award-winning poet, she was coordinator of the Tidewater Writers Association for ten years, and the Christopher Newport University Annual Writers Conference for four years. She also taught poetry for their Lifelong Learning Center. Christine continues to write, while reading extensively.

Martha W. Steger is a native of Accomack County on Virginia's Eastern Shore. She was Public Relations Director for the state's tourism office for more than twenty-five years, after being Senior Editor of *Richmond LifeStyle Magazine.* She is a free-lance writer with journalistic articles, essays, poems, and short stories to her credit.

Judith Stevens has been writing since the second grade. She delights in tramping the woods with poet-husband Jack Callan and co-hosting events in area museums, coffeehouses, libraries, and schools. A Norfolk resident working in Virginia Beach as a Wellness Director at First Colonial Inn, she crafted the senior Creative Writing Program there and delights in introducing poetry to people of all ages.

Sydney Sylvester is a junior at Appomattox Regional Governor's School for the Arts and Technology. His poems have been published in *Asgard* and have won Silver Keys in *Scholastic.* One of his poems also was awarded second place in the Jenkins Prize competition of the Poetry Society of Virginia.

Andrea T. was born and raised in Minnesota and is working toward a Ph.D. degree in Environmental Engineering at Virginia Tech. She hopes to become a professor at a smaller university or liberal arts college. She enjoys cooking, music, and time spent outdoors.

Guy Terrell holds a Master's degree in Information Systems and works as a Project Manager in Information Technology. He assisted with the production of a DVD of Virginia Poets Laureate from 1996-2004, under the auspices of the Poetry Society of Virginia, of which he is the current President. He has had poems published in *Streetlight* and *Tar River Poetry.*

Vivian Teter teaches at Virginia Wesleyan College. Her work includes the collection *Translating a Bridge* and poems in *Spoon River, The Missouri Review, Poetry East, The Gettysburg Review, Green Mountains Review* and other journals. She has received two Pushcart Prize nominations and several fellowships from the Virginia Center for the Creative Arts.

Graham West Thomas, four years old, lives in Carrollton, Virginia. His favorite activities are playing with friends and legos, swimming, climbing, running, and hearing stories and poems. "Grandma" **Mary Jean Kledzik**, a widely published poet, lives in Norfolk and is the volunteer story-time reader at Graham's KinderCare. She and her husband enjoy friends, volunteer work, reading, and traveling.

Dr. John Urquhart and Elizabeth Urquhart are retired teachers living in Hampton. Elizabeth writes poetry and is interested in gardening, music, and wildlife. Her husband John taught mathematics and computer science and now is an official poet's helper. They live happily with five cats raised from feral kittens and enjoy watching possums, squirrels, egrets, and herons in their yard.

John Graves Warner is a filmmaker living in the North End of Virginia Beach; he has just completed the feature film *Knight of the Gun*. From 1991 to 2010, he was the co-creator and managing producer of the program *Virginia Currents* on public television.

Marguerite Thoburn Watkins was born and went to boarding school in the foothills of the Himalayas, growing up there and in Jabalpur, Central India. She attended Bates College in Maine, married Gordon Watkins, a Virginian, and has spent fifty-nine years in Lynchburg. She taught handicapped children but is now retired. A grandmother of ten, she enjoys writing, reading, hiking, identifying birds and flowers, and traveling.

Jill M. Winkowski currently works as a technical writer. She has worked as a freelance reporter, a magazine editor, an educator, and an analyst. Her undergraduate degrees are in English and German, and her graduate degree is in Applied Linguistics. She is active in the writing community of the Hampton Roads area of Virginia.

Tucker Withers, his wife Mary Ann, and their three children operate the Little River Inn, a six-room bed and breakfast in the quaint village of Aldie, Virginia (www.aldie.com). A short walk away is their antique shop. Since childhood trips to Williamsburg, Tucker has had a keen interest in history, architecture, art, antiques, and travel.

Bob Young is a retired social worker, teacher, psychotherapist, war resister, and body surfer. From 1973 to 1991, he was Associate Professor at the Eastern Virginia Medical School Department of Psychiatry. His book of poems, *If Not Now, When*, was published in 2011. He has won awards from the Poetry Society of Virginia and the Christopher Newport University Writers Conference.

Lauvonda Lynn M. Young is an award-winning writer and poet, the author of *Just A Woman* (poetry) and other published works. She spent most of her career at the University of Virginia (Charlottesville), with job responsibilities including human resource management, supervision, geriatric grant administration, and special event planning and organization.

Alexander (Alexandros) G. Zestos was born in Bloomington, Indiana, and grew up in Williamsburg. His family is originally from Thessaly, Greece, and he currently resides in Charlottesville, where he is a Ph.D. candidate in Chemistry at the University of Virginia. His interests include research, travel, culture, and sports.

Index

Names of readers appear in regular font; titles of poems and names of poets appear in *italics*.

Acknowledgments

Every effort has been made to identify, locate, and secure permission wherever necessary from those who hold rights to the poems in this anthology. Any omitted acknowledgments brought to the editor's attention will be added to future editions. The editor may be reached directly through her website, www.sofiamstarnes.com.

"Why Then Do We Not Despair" from POEMS OF AKHMATOVA, selected, translated, and introduced by Stanley Kunitz with Max Hayward (Mariner Books, Houghton Mifflin Harcourt). Translation © 1973 by Stanley Kunitz and Max Hayward. Translation used by permission of the Estate of Stanley Kunitz c/o Darhansoff & Verrill Literary Agents. All rights reserved.

"Variations on the Word Love" by Margaret Atwood. Copyright © Margaret Atwood. Reprinted by permission of The Lamore Literary Agency, on behalf of Margaret Atwood.

"For My Children, Each of You" from LEANING TO HEAR THE MUSIC by Joseph Awad. Copyright © Joseph Awad, Road Publishers, 1997. Reprinted by permission of Doris Awad.

"Heaven on Earth" by Kristin Berkey-Abbott. Copyright © 2003 by Kristin Berkey-Abbott. First appeared in *Coal City Review*, published also in WHISTLING PAST THE GRAVEYARD, Pudding House Press, 2004. Reprinted by permission of the author.

"Ithaca" by Constantine Cavafy. Translation accessed from Wikipedia. Constantine Cavafy, on Wikipedia: http://en.wikipedia.org/wiki/Cavafy, available under the Creative Commons Attribution-ShareAlike License Agreement.

"if i should" by Lucille Clifton from THE BOOK OF LIGHT. Copyright © 1993 by Lucille Clifton.

CPSIA information can be obtained
at www.ICGtesting.com
Printed in the USA
FFOW04n1223130214
3595FF